B2 Listening

Cambridge Masterclass

Fiona Aish and Jo Tomlinson

© Prosperity Education Ltd. 2024

Registered offices: Sherlock Close, Cambridge
CB3 0HP, United Kingdom

First published 2024

ISBN: 978-1-915654-22-9

This publication is in copyright. Subject to statutory exception
and to the provisions of relevant collective licensing agreements,
no reproduction of any part may take place without the written
permission of Prosperity Education.

The moral rights of the authors have been asserted.

'Cambridge B2 First' and 'FCE' are brands
belonging to The Chancellor, Masters and Scholars of the
University of Cambridge and are not associated with
Prosperity Education or its products.

Designed by ORP Cambridge

Audio produced by FFG Audio

Producer: David Pickering; Actors: Rob and Natalie Holman,
Jessica Bennett, Sandy Murray, and Jake and Rhiana Drake

For further information and resources, visit:
www.prosperityeducation.net

To infinity and beyond.

To download the audio content:

Go to www.prosperityeducation.net/downloads
Enter password: TIAB
Select the book image
Select content to download

Contents

Introduction — 5

Part 1 Multiple choice — 9

Part 2 Sentence completion — 15

Part 3 Multiple matching — 21

Part 4 Multiple choice — 25

Answers and transcripts — 31

Practice tests — 63

Practice test transcripts — 96

Practice test answers — 120

Fiona Aish and **Jo Tomlinson** are directors of Target English, a consultancy that provides tailor-made solutions in content creation, course provision, training and testing. They have co-written several leading titles in English exam preparation, and create materials and assessment resources for a range of educational providers. They are DELTA-qualified and hold MAs in ELT and Applied Linguistics and Language Testing, respectively.

Introduction

Cambridge B2 First Listening

Welcome to this book on the Cambridge B2 First Listening paper. B2 First is one of the exams in the series provided by Cambridge Assessment – part of the University of Cambridge. It is the second in the range of tests they provide in General English:

A2	Key (KET)
B1	Preliminary (PET)
B2	First (FCE)
C1	Advanced (CAE)
C2	Proficiency (CPE)

The references next to each test refer to the CEFR Level (Common European Framework of Reference), and show the language level of each test. For CEFR B2 Listening, you will need to be able to:

- understand the topic or the purpose of the extract
- identify the overall meaning of the extract or specific details
- identify how speakers feel or their attitude towards a topic or situation
- understand when two speakers agree or disagree.

How does the test work?

You can take the B2 First exam on a computer or on paper. The content is the same for both forms of the test. The Listening section of the B2 First examination gives you the opportunity to show your comprehension ability by following a range of spoken materials, including news programmes, presentations and everyday conversations.

The B2 First Listening paper consists of the following:

Time allowed	40 minutes
Number of parts	4
Number of questions	Part 1: eight multiple-choice questions Part 2: ten sentence-completion questions Part 3: eight multiple-matching questions Part 4: seven multiple-choice questions

Part 1: Multiple choice

This first part of the B2 First Listening examination consists of eight short extracts, which could be monologues or dialogues. Each extract has one multiple-choice question with three options: A, B or C. There is one mark for each correct answer. You will listen to each extract twice. These questions test your ability to:

> understand the topic or the purpose of the extract; identify the overall meaning of the extract or specific details; ide tify how speakers feel or their attitude towards a topic or situation; understand when two speakers agree or disagree.

Part 2: Sentence completion

The second part of the B2 First Listening examination consists of one longer extract of 3–4 minutes, which is a monologue. You must complete ten sentences about this extract. Complete the gaps with words you hear on the recording. There is one mark for each correct answer. You will listen to each extract twice. These questions test your ability to:

> understand detail; identify specific in ormation; identify the speaker's opinion; follow longer speech.

Part 3: Multiple matching

Part 3 of the B2 First Listening examination consists of five short monologues of about 30 seconds. All the speakers will talk about the same topic but from a different point of view. You have to match what each speaker says to a list of options. There are eight options so three are not needed. There is one mark for each correct answer. You will listen to each extract twice. These questions test your ability to:

> understand detail; identify specific in ormation; understand different speakers; identify different opinions and feelings.

Part 4: Multiple choice

The final part of the B2 First Listening examination consists of one longer extract of 3–4 minutes, which is a dialogue between two speakers. There are seven multiple-choice questions about the extract. These will follow the order of the information you hear. The questions each have three options: A, B or C. There is one mark for each correct answer. You will listen to each extract twice. These questions test your ability to:

> understand main ideas and identify specific in ormation; identify the speaker's opinion and attitude; follow longer speech.

How to use this book

The main section of this book focuses on each Listening task type individually, explaining its characteristics and providing guidance on how to plan a response to an example question. There follow several exam-styled practice tests with detailed answer keys and commentary.

Each unit contains the following sections:

- **Prepare:** This section introduces the question type, describes what you are are being tested on and gives you guidance and detailed suggestions to help you do well.

- **Practise:** To prepare you for taking on an exam-styled text and questions, each unit contains a series of practice exercises with detailed answer keys that clarify how and why answers are correct. These exercises are shorter than the real exam, but follow the same format.

- **Put it to the test:** Next there are two full-length exam-styled texts with questions. Again, there are detailed answer keys. You will find these keys especially helpful as they explain why the correct answers are correct as well as point out why you may have chosen incorrect answers (such as 'distractors').

Answers and transcripts

Detailed answers to questions for each unit are provided along with full transcripts of each audio recording.

Practice tests

The resource contains an additional four B2 First Listening practice tests (Parts 1–4) with transcripts and answer keys.

Audio download

To access or download the audio content, visit:

www.prosperityeducation.net/downloads

- Enter password: **TIAB**
- Select book image
- Select content to access/download

Prosperity Education Ltd.
Cambridge, CB3 0HP
United Kingdom

Dear Customer,

Thank you for buying from us.

If you like our resources and what we do, please help us get our story out there.

	You can follow Prosperity Education (and in fact any of your favourite authors) on **Amazon**.	
	Our **website** contains lots of free exam-practice materials and sample downloads.	
	Our **Facebook** page regularly posts English language quizzes, discount codes and free stu˜.	
	Follow our **Instagram** stories for updates on our English teaching and learning resources.	
	Subscribe to our **Youtube** channel for Listening, Speaking and Writing practice and tutorials.	

I wish you all the very best for your studies.

Tom O'Reilly, Founder of Prosperity Education

Part 1: Multiple choice

B2 First Listening

Prepare

This first part of the B2 First Listening examination consists of eight short extracts, which could be monologues or dialogues. Each extract has one multiple-choice question with three options: A, B or C. There is one mark for each correct answer. You will listen to each extract **twice**. These questions test your ability to:

- understand the topic or the purpose of the extract
- identify the overall meaning of the extract or specific details
- identify how speakers feel or their attitude towards a topic or situation
- understand when two speakers agree or disagree.

Suggestions to help you do well in this task

Before you listen

- Read the questions carefully. They will tell you the contexts of the listening extracts and what information you are listening for.
- Focus on the options. When you read the options, underline the key words and notice the differences between each option.
- Be prepared to hear some or all the options, either directly or indirectly.

While you listen

- Choose the option (A, B or C) that you think is correct. Check your answer by trying to rule out the other two options. You will have a second chance to listen to the extracts and check your answer.
- Move on to the next question. If you find one question very hard, don't spend too much time thinking about it.
- Don't be distracted by the other options. Remember, extracts will contain **distractors** – pieces of information that may lead you towards choosing the wrong answer. The way to avoid becoming distracted or 'tricked' is to read the questions and options very carefully and listen for the exact information required by the question. Do not just select the first option you hear mentioned; remember, it must answer the question.

Have a go at some practice questions on the following pages.

B2 Listening | Cambridge Masterclass

Practise 1

You are going to hear two listening extracts. **Before** you listen to the audio, read the questions below and underline the key words in the questions and options.

Ask yourself:

- How are the questions and options in Questions 1 and 2 different?
- Can you think of any other ways of saying these options?

1. You hear two friends talking about going to a theme park. What is the woman annoyed about?

    A   the prices
    B   the rides
    C   the queues

2. You hear a man talking about traffic in the city. He thinks that the council should:

    A   extend the area covered by public transport.
    B   charge car drivers to enter the city centre.
    C   limit the city centre to pedestrians only.

Practise 2

Now listen to the audio and read the extracts for Questions 1 and 2. Select the correct answer A, B or C. Then:

- highlight the part of the extract where you identified the answer
- underline parts of the extracts connected to the distracting options.

Extract 1

Man	You went to Splash World at the weekend, didn't you? Did you have a good time? My kids love it there.
Woman	We normally love a theme park too, but it could have been better to be honest. We decided to go as it's low season and we thought the queues would be smaller. Well, that was true, but only half the rides were working! The ones my eldest wanted to go on were all under maintenance.
Man	Really? You'd think they'd reduce the ticket prices for that!
Woman	Well, any theme park is pretty expensive these days. We still made the best of it.

Extract 2

The council really needs to take action on the traffic – it's awful these days. I know some city councils have introduced those systems where people pay if they're coming into the city centre, but I'm not sure that would work personally. I'd rather have a completely traffic-free zone, even for the buses. I don't see why the council can't make this happen. Especially as it's cheap compared to other options. The issue for me, of course, is that I can't get a bus from where I live. It's about five kilometres from the city, but I tend to cycle most places so it's not a big problem.

Practise 3

 1_P_3

Now you are going to listen to four more extracts. For Questions 3–6, choose the correct answer A, B or C.

3. You hear part of a conversation between two friends. What are they talking about?

   A   Moving house
   B   A family celebration
   C   Going on holiday

4. You hear a woman leaving an answerphone message. Why is she calling?

   A   To confirm some details
   B   To postpone something
   C   To ask for assistance

5. You hear two people discussing what they did at the weekend. What do they both say about the campsite?

   A   The management was impressive.
   B   The setting was picturesque.
   C   The facilities were adequate.

6. You hear two people talking about a concert. They agree that:

   A   the sound quality was poor.
   B   the venue was too crowded.
   C   the band were disappointing.

Answers and transcripts on pages 32–35

B2 Listening | Cambridge Masterclass

Put it to the test 1

You will hear people talking in eight different situations. For Questions 1–8, choose the correct answer, A, B or C.

1. You hear two parents talking about their children's football match. How does the woman feel about the match?

   A The final result was unfair.
   B One team played badly.
   C It was an exciting match.

2. You hear a news story on local radio. What is the purpose of the announcement?

   A To promote an event
   B To recommend an activity
   C To support a proposal

3. You hear part of a conversation between a customer and a tourist office assistant. What does the woman want to know about?

   A Train times
   B Airport transfers
   C Bus tours

4. You hear a station announcement about a delayed train. Passengers who want to go to Manchester should:

   A wait for information.
   B buy a new ticket.
   C take another train.

5. You hear two friends talking about booking tickets. They agree to:

   A wait until later.
   B get them in person.
   C sit separately.

6. You hear a gardener talking about his work. What does he dislike about his job?

   A The salary is quite low.
   B The work is unpredictable.
   C The schedule is exhausting.

Part 1 | Multiple Choice | Put it to the test

7. You hear two friends talking about online shopping. What annoys the man?

   A Poor products
   B Slow payment
   C Delivery charges

8. You hear a teacher talking to her students. What is she telling them about?

   A Changes to exam dates.
   B Arrangements for a trip.
   C An important email.

Watch out for **distractors** – information that may lead to choosing a wrong answer!

Put it to the test 2

You will hear people talking in eight different situations. For Questions 1–8, choose the correct answer, A, B or C.

1. You hear two people talking about an art exhibition. What do they agree about?

   A The artist was brilliant.
   B It needed more artworks.
   C The works were confusing.

2. You hear two people talking about buying a new car. What is important for the woman?

   A Brand
   B Size
   C Cost

3. You hear a tour guide talking about a city. Why does he recommend the old town?

   A To hear traditional music.
   B To eat cheaply.
   C To see great architecture.

Answers and transcripts on pages 35–42

4. You hear part of an interview with an actor. How did he get started in his career?

   A He met a director by chance.
   B He was hired by an agency.
   C He applied for a lot of roles.

5. You will hear a man leaving an answerphone message. What is the main reason for his message?

   A To promise something
   B To blame someone
   C To praise somewhere

6. You hear two people talking about changes in their town. What does the woman think about the art gallery?

   A It is a positive addition to the town.
   B It will be welcomed by residents.
   C It has changed the look of the town.

7. You hear two people talking about a trip. What are they discussing?

   A The transport
   B The accommodation
   C The day trips

8. You hear a student talking about finishing her university course. How does she feel about the experience?

   A It made her more realistic.
   B It was too competitive.
   C It changed her work goals.

Part 2: Sentence completion

Prepare

The second part of the B2 First Listening examination consists of one longer extract of 3–4 minutes, which is a monologue. You must complete ten sentences about this extract. Complete the gaps with words you hear on the recording. There is one mark for each correct answer. You will listen to each extract **twice**. These questions test your ability to:

- understand detail
- identify specific information
- identify the speaker's opinion
- follow longer speech.

Suggestions to help you do well in this task

Before you listen

- Read the sentences carefully. They will tell you the context of the listening extract and what information you are listening for. Notice important information in the sentences that can lead you to the correct answer.
- Underline key words in the sentence. This will help you identify a correct answer.
- Focus on the gaps. Look at the grammar of the sentence and try to identify what kind of word can complete the gap (e.g. noun, verb or adjective). Many are nouns.
- Think of possible answers to complete the gap. What answers would make sense in the sentence?

While you listen

- Note down the answers you think complete the gaps. Only use words you hear. **Do not** change any words.
- Use the underlined key words to keep moving through the questions. If you find one question very hard, or do not hear the answer, leave it and move on. Remember, you will hear the extract twice.
- You might hear some distracting information. Remember that the words must match grammatically and agree with **all** the information in the sentence.
- Don't write too much. Answers will be no more than three words in length.

Have a go at some practice questions on the following pages.

B2 Listening | Cambridge Masterclass

Practise 1

You are going to hear a man called Nick talking about training to be a chef. **Before** you listen to the audio, read the sentences (1–4) below and underline the key words.

Ask yourself:

- What kind of words need to go into the gaps?
- What clues in the sentences help you know what kind of word completes the gaps?
- What words seem possible or likely?

Nick was originally interested in being a (1)_____Lawyer_____.   noun – job: doctor, teacher, police officer?

While he was at university, Nick worked at a (2)_____.

Nick's (3)_____ were pleased that he decided to be a chef.

Doing a college course gave Nick some (4)_____ for cookery.

Practise 2

 2_P_2

Now listen to the audio and read the following extract for sentences 1–4. Complete the sentences with a word or short phrase. Then:

- highlight the part of the extract where you identified the answer
- underline parts of the extract connected to the distracting options.

Extract 1

Hello. My name is Nick, and I'm going to tell you all about what it takes to be a chef. Now, I didn't always want to be a chef, but I was always interested in food. You see, my dad is a farmer and I grew up helping out a lot. But actually I wanted to be a lawyer. It sounded much more exciting!

It all changed when I went to university, though, and I started cooking my own food. I found that more interesting than my degree course. I used to study during the day and then get cooking books out of the library to find out more about it. I did all that while helping out at a bike shop… and I spent everything that I made there on trying new foods.

I decided at the end of my degree that I wanted to be a chef. It was a bit of a shock for my parents, who thought I had wasted my time at university, but my housemates were really

supportive of me. But they had tasted the food I'd learnt to cook, and they knew I had talent.

So, I started looking for training courses. I could have done another degree, but I wanted practical experience in a kitchen. I ended up doing a part-time course and also working as an apprentice chef part-time too. I picked up lots of basic skills on the course, like working with meat and how to store foods, and I learnt creativity and speed in the restaurant.

Practise 3

 2_P_3

Now you are going to listen to the rest of the extract. For Sentences 5–10, complete the sentences with a word or short phrase.

Nick thinks that the **(5)**_____ is the hardest thing about being a chef.

At first, Nick couldn't add much **(6)**_____ to his dishes.

Nick thinks the best dish on the menu is the **(7)**_____.

Nick tries to avoid making **(8)**_____ if he can.

The approach of **(9)**_____ makes Nick's restaurant different from others.

Nick recommends gaining some **(10)**_____ as a first step into being a chef.

Answers and transcripts on pages 42–44

B2 Listening | Cambridge Masterclass

Put it to the test 1

 2_T_1

You will hear a woman called Grace from the tourist office talking about a Scottish Island. For Questions 1–10, complete the sentences with a word or short phrase.

Grace thinks the best thing about the island is the **(1)**_____.

Visitors can often view different types of **(2)**_____ from the boat.

After some people going to **(3)**_____ stopped at the island, it became famous.

(4)_____ are too large to get into the cave.

Its alternative name probably comes from a visit by a **(5)**_____.

The **(6)**_____ caused the only people living on the island to leave.

The only building on the island is a **(7)**_____.

The island is now owned by a **(8)**_____.

You can walk up to the **(9)**_____ during the tours.

It's a good idea to look at the **(10)**_____ before going on a tour.

Put it to the test 2

 2_T_2

You will hear a man called Martin Jackson talking about a community garden he helped to create. For Questions 1–10, complete the sentences with a word or short phrase.

The residents in Martin's block of flats wanted the garden to be used for (1)_____.

Adding some (2)_____ will make the community garden brighter and more attractive.

The residents (3)_____ the various jobs that need doing in the garden.

Martin was surprised that he needed a lot of (4)_____ to do the spraying.

The covered (5)_____ means that people can be in the garden all year round.

Martin noticed that residents (6)_____ differently because of the garden.

Community gardens in cities highlight the importance of (7)_____ and connection.

It is common to see gardens on (8)_____ and public buildings.

Martin points out that the roofs of city buildings are often (9)_____.

The residents might invest in (10)_____ so they can use rainwater in the garden.

Answers and transcripts on pages 44–48

B2 First Listening

Part 3: Multiple matching

Prepare

Part 3 of the B2 First Listening examination consists of five short monologues, each lasting about 30 seconds. All the speakers will talk about the same topic but from a different point of view. You have to match what each speaker says to a list of options. There are eight options so three are not needed. There is one mark for each correct answer. You will listen to each extract **twice**.

These questions test your ability to:

- understand detail
- identify specific information
- understand different speakers
- identify different opinions and feelings.

Suggestions to help you do well in this task

Before you listen

- Read the instructions carefully. They will tell you the general topic of the monologues **and** what kind of information you are listening for.
- Underline the topic and the question or specific information you need to focus on.
- Underline key words in the options. Notice how the options are different and what specific details are presented in each of the options.
- Think about what synonyms you might hear on the recording.

While you listen

- Wait until the end of each monologue before you choose your answer. The speakers will mention some of the key words in more than one of the options, but only one option will match **exactly**.
- Remember that you will hear the extract twice, so as you listen for the first time make a note of the possible answers.
- When you listen for the second time, choose the answer you are most sure about.
- Listen for synonyms and different ways to say the information in the options.

Have a go at some practice questions on the following pages.

B2 Listening | Cambridge Masterclass

Practise 1

Before you listen to the audio, read the instructions and options below. Underline the question in the instruction and the key words in the options.

Ask yourself:

- What does the question focus on?
- Can you think of any other ways to say the options?

Next, you will hear two short extracts in which people are talking about practising a sport. For Questions 1 and 2, choose from the list (A–H), the main goal of each speaker. Use the letters only once. There are three extra letters that you do not need to use.

A   to train with other people more

B   to increase their physical strength

C   to become more sociable

D   to strengthen their determination

E   to implement a routine

F   to win a competition

G   to improve a specific technique

H   to manage stress from work

Speaker 1: [1]

Speaker 2: [2]

Practise 2

🎧 3_P_2

Now listen to the audio and read the following extracts for Questions 1 and 2. Choose from the list (A–H) the main goal of each speaker. Then:

- highlight the part of the extract where you identified the answer
- underline parts of the extracts connected to the distracting options.

Extract 1

I'm training for a marathon next year. I don't think it will be too difficult because I've run some 10K races before. I'm quite self-motivated and have created my own schedule: I run three times a week before work and then once at the weekend with my running club. But the thing I'm a little bit concerned about is whether I'm strong enough. I'm going to need to spend a lot more time in the gym doing weights and exercises to build up my leg muscles. At the moment they're good for short distances, but I have to change this if I want to actually finish a marathon.

Extract 2

I took up yoga last year because I work long hours at a computer and was suffering from hip pain. At first, I found it hard to build time for yoga into my daily life. I was always distracted by something. I decided to join a class, which gave me some structure, and the classes started to make a difference – and now I feel more motivated to do it at home. I aim to plan my home yoga sessions at the beginning of each week and make sure that nothing gets in the way. I've got quite a busy and stressful life, but I'm sure I can devote time to it.

Practise 3

 3_P_3

Now, you will hear the final three speakers. For Questions 3–5, choose from the list (A–H) the main goal of each speaker.

- **A** to train with other people more
- **B** to increase their physical strength
- **C** to become more sociable
- **D** to strengthen their determination
- **E** to implement a routine
- **F** to win a competition
- **G** to improve a specific technique
- **H** to manage stress from work

Speaker 3: [3]
Speaker 4: [4]
Speaker 5: [5]

Answers and transcripts on pages 48–50

B2 Listening | Cambridge Masterclass

Put it to the test 1

 3_T_1

You will hear five short extracts in which people talking about travelling by plane. For Questions 1–5, choose from the list (A–H) what each person feels about it. Use the letters only once. There are three extra letters that you do not need to use.

A Thinks it's too complicated

B Enjoys the sense of adventure

C Makes them feel nervous

D Prefers flying alone

E Finds it uncomfortable

F Likes the service

G Enjoys the luxury

H Likes looking out the window

Speaker 1: [1]
Speaker 2: [2]
Speaker 3: [3]
Speaker 4: [4]
Speaker 5: [5]

Put it to the test 2

 3_T_2

You will hear five short extracts in which people talking about their first day at school. For Questions 1–5, choose from the list (A–H) each person's strongest memory. Use the letters only once. There are three extra letters that you do not need to use.

A The worry of being a new student

B The assistance from the staff

C The design of the building

D The excitement of making friends

E The personality of their teacher

F The equipment in their classroom

G The number of people

H The range of fun activities

Speaker 1: [1]
Speaker 2: [2]
Speaker 3: [3]
Speaker 4: [4]
Speaker 5: [5]

Answers and transcripts on pages 51–53

Part 4: Multiple choice

B2 First Listening

Prepare

The final part of the B2 First Listening examination consists of one longer extract of 3–4 minutes, which is a dialogue between two speakers. There are seven multiple-choice questions about the extract. These will follow the order of the information you hear. The questions each have three options: A, B or C. There is one mark for each correct answer. You will listen to each extract **twice**. These questions test your ability to:

- understand main ideas and identify specific information
- identify the speaker's opinion and attitude
- follow longer speech.

Suggestions to help you do well in this task

Before you listen

- Read all the questions. They will tell you the context of the listening extract, what kind of information you are listening for and how the conversation will develop.
- Underline key words in the questions.
- Focus on the options. When you read the options, underline the key words and notice the differences between each option.
- Be prepared to hear some or all the options, either directly or indirectly. But remember that only one option answers the question correctly.

While you listen

- Choose the option (A, B or C) that you think is correct. Check your answer by trying to rule out the other two options.
- If you find one question hard, don't spend too much time thinking about it. Remember to move on to the next question as the subject changes.
- Don't be distracted by the other options. Remember, extracts will contain **distractors** – pieces of information that may lead you towards choosing the wrong answer. The way to avoid becoming distracted is to read the questions and options very carefully and listen for the exact information required by the question. Do not just select the first option you hear mentioned, remember it must answer the question.

Have a go at some practice questions on the following pages.

B2 Listening | Cambridge Masterclass

Practise 1

You will hear an interview with Alex Blakely, who manages a summer camp, talking about the benefits for teenagers.

Before you listen to the audio, read Questions 1–3 and underline the key words:

1. Alex believes summer camps are a good experience because:

    A   they only last a short time.
    B   the staff are well qualified.
    C   there is a range of activities on offer.

2. How are summer camps different from school?

    A   They have more activities.
    B   They are more flexible.
    C   They focus more on skills.

3. What does Alex say teenagers develop on the camp?

    A   Leadership skills
    B   Independence
    C   Self confidence

Now tick (✓) the points in the list (A–F) that you think will be included in the interview. Which parts of the questions helped you decide?

    A   Things that teenagers learn on summer camps   ☐
    B   A description of different types of summer camp   ☐
    C   Why teenagers prefer summer camps to school   ☐
    D   How to help teenagers who get homesick   ☐
    E   A comparison with school activities   ☐
    F   Advantages of attending a summer camp   ☐

Practise 2

 4_P_2

Now listen to the audio and read the extract for Questions 1–3. Choose the correct answer and then:

- highlight the part of the extract where you identified the answer
- underline parts of the extract connected to the distracting options.

Part 4 | Multiple choice | Practise

Extract 1

Interviewer   I'm joined this morning by Alex Blakely, manager of the UK's largest summer camp. He believes that all parents should seriously consider sending their teenagers on a summer camp. So, tell us Alex, why are you convinced that this is such as great idea?

Alex   Hello. Well, for me it's about opening their eyes to new things. In their daily lives, teenagers might go to a dance class or play a sport, or attend a weekly group like Scouts. But here they're able to try out so many things they've never done before. Our staff have a lot of experience working with young people, and we really want them to make the most of their time with us. After all, most participants only spend two or three weeks at camp.

Interviewer   Some parents don't want to pay for an experience that they feel is similar to school. What is your opinion on this?

Alex   Even though the teenagers are a similar age, and the activities are all learning experiences, summer camps are unique. This is because there is a lot more freedom. We don't have a prescribed programme. Also, we encourage participants to get involved with as many or as few activities as they want.

Interviewer   What skills do teenagers learn at the camp?

Alex   At this age, young people are developing their identity quite rapidly. We're keen to show them ways to do this successfully. Although they cannot be fully in charge of their day-to-day lives, we want them to grow as people. Positive learning experiences at the camp make students see their abilities more clearly.

Practise 3

 4_P_3

Now you are going to listen to the rest of the extract. For Questions 4–7, choose the best answer (A, B or C).

4. What do the camp counsellors help teenagers do?

     A   Solve friendship issues

     B   Be more emotional

     C   Learn how to argue

5. Why are teenagers not allowed mobile phones at the camp?

     A   To help them rely on technology less

     B   To prevent contact with their parents

     C   To improve communication skills

Answers and transcripts on pages 54–56

6. When choosing a summer camp, parents prefer places that:

   A are convenient to get to.
   B offer water sports.
   C other parents recommend.

7. After summer camp, parents often report that their children:

   A keep the house tidier.
   B get up earlier in the morning.
   C organise themselves better.

> Watch out for **distractors** – information that may lead to choosing a wrong answer!

Put it to the test 1

You will hear part of an interview with Victoria Bradshaw, who works as a vet, talking about the challenges and rewards of her job. For Questions 1–7, choose the best answer (A, B or C).

1. What does Victoria say about studying to be a vet?

   A It was harder than she expected.
   B She adapted to the course demands.
   C It was a rewarding experience.

2. According to Victoria, team meetings help the vets:

   A deal with stressful situations.
   B make decisions more quickly.
   C come up with new approaches.

3. Why is talking to pet owners difficult for vets?

   A They are very emotional.
   B They can be unpredictable.
   C They want positive news.

> Answers ad transcripts on pages 56–58

Part 4 | Multiple choice | Put it to the test

4. Working as a farm vet helped Victoria to:

   A rely on her knowledge.
   B improve her communication.
   C manage her schedule.

5. What did Victoria admire about farmers?

   A Their approach to animals' health issues.
   B The way they communicate with vets.
   C How they care for their animals.

6. Victoria thinks that managing a veterinary practice:

   A is something she would like to do one day.
   B could become boring after a while.
   C would not be the best use of her skills.

7. How has technology affected Victoria's job?

   A The paperwork has been reduced.
   B The practice has more customers.
   C The staff have become more efficient.

Put it to the test 2

4_T_2

You will hear part of an interview with Tom Lawrence, a chess player. For Questions 1–7, choose the best answer (A, B or C).

1. Tom started playing chess because:

   A he liked intellectual games.
   B he wanted to please his parents.
   C he had friends in a local club.

2. The thing that most interests Tom about chess is that:

   A it involves a lot of luck.
   B there are many strategies.
   C each game is unique.

Answers and transcripts on pages 59–61

3. What do chess players begin to understand as they improve their skills?

    A That it's more difficult than it appears
    B That the rules are complicated
    C That losing is good for learning

4. What are the benefits of playing chess for the brain?

    A Improved intelligence
    B Better overall function
    C More creative thinking

5. What does Tom say about chess books?

    A They help beginners get started.
    B They are not worth the money.
    C They are useful for advanced players.

6. Tom thinks that chess remains popular because:

    A people of different ages like playing it.
    B there are so many opportunities to play it.
    C it is part of many cultures around the world.

7. What is Tom's assessment of playing chess against a computer?

    A It prepares players for competitions.
    B It provides limited practice.
    C It gives a wide range of practice.

Answers and transcripts on pages 59–61

Answers

Part 1: Multiple choice | pages 32–42

Practise *32*

Put it to the test 1 *35*

Put it to the test 2 *38*

Part 2: Sentence matching | pages 42–48

Practise *42*

Put it to the test 1 *44*

Put it to the test 2 *46*

Part 3: Multiple matching | pages 48–53

Practise *48*

Put it to the test 1 *51*

Put it to the test 2 *52*

Part 4: Multiple choice | pages 54–61

Practise *54*

Put it to the test 1 *57*

Put it to the test 2 *59*

B2 Listening | Cambridge Masterclass

Part 1: Practise 1 | Answers   (page 10)

1. You hear two friends talking about going to a theme park. What is the woman annoyed about?

   A the prices
   B the rides
   C the queues

   Question 1 is a direct question. The options are all short.
   prices – money to get in, cost, entrance fee, pay, amount
   rides – attractions
   queues – waiting times, lines

2. You hear a man talking about traffic in the city. He thinks that the council should:

   A extend the area covered by public transport
   B charge car drivers to enter the city centre
   C limit the city centre to pedestrians only.

   extend – increase, spread, make bigger
   area – zone, space
   public transport – buses, trains, trams
   charge – ask for money, pay
   car drivers – motorists, vehicle owners
   limit – stop, reduce,
   pedestrians – people walking, people on foot

   Question 2 requires you to complete the sentence with an option. The options are all longer and parts of a complete sentence.

Part 1: Practise 2 | Answers   (pages 10–11)

1. You hear two friends talking about going to a theme park. What is the woman annoyed about?

   A the prices
   B the rides ✓
   C the queues

Transcript

Man	You went to Splash World at the weekend, didn't you? Did you have a good time? My kids love it there.
Woman	We normally love a theme park too, but it could have been better to be honest. We decided to go as it's low season and we thought the queues would be smaller. Well, that was true, but only half the rides were working! The ones my eldest wanted to go on were all under maintenance.
Man	Really? You'd think they'd reduce the ticket prices for that!
Woman	Well, any theme park is pretty expensive these days. We still made the best of it.

32

Part 1 | Answers

2. You hear a man talking about traffic in the city. He thinks that the council should:

   A   extend the area covered by public transport.
   B   charge car drivers to enter the city centre.
   C   limit the city centre to pedestrians only.

Transcript

The council really needs to take action on the traffic – it's awful these days. I know some city councils have introduced those systems where people pay if they're coming into the city centre, but I'm not sure that would work personally. I'd rather have a completely traffic-free zone, even for the buses. I don't see why the council can't make this happen. Especially as it's cheap compared to other options. The issue for me, of course, is that I can't get a bus from where I live. It's about five kilometres from the city, but I tend to cycle most places so it's not a big problem.

Part 1: Practise 3 | Answers (page 11)

3. You hear part of a conversation between two friends. What are they talking about?

   A   Moving house
   B   A family celebration
   C   Going on holiday

Transcript

Woman	You know, I could really do with a holiday, but I don't think that'll happen any time soon.
Man	Oh, I know the feeling! But what's wrong?
Woman	I'm just so exhausted after all the preparations for our move. It's taken ages for all the paperwork to be completed, and this last week I've had to help the children pack up all their belongings.
Man	You know, moving is such a big life event for all the family that I'm not surprised you feel like you need a break. Hopefully you can celebrate when you've unpacked.

4. You hear a woman leaving an answerphone message. Why is she calling?

   A   To confirm some details
   B   To postpone something
   C   To ask for assistance

Transcript

Hi there, Tom. I hope you haven't left the house already. I just wanted to let you know that the match has been called off because Andy's broken down on the motorway and he's got all the equipment with him. He's called the mechanic for help, but who knows how long that will take, so, we've got nothing to play with! I'm sure everyone will be disappointed, but there's just nothing we can do. Hopefully, we'll be able to play at the same time tomorrow instead, as long as the pitch is free and it doesn't rain. Does tomorrow at ten thirty work for you?

5. You hear two people discussing what they did at the weekend. What do they both say about the campsite?

- **A** The management was impressive.
- **B** The setting was picturesque.
- **C** The facilities were adequate.

Transcript

Woman	Would you go back to that campsite, Tony?
Man	Oh, absolutely. I mean, it was worth it just for the sunsets over the hills. They've chosen a great spot there, although the showers would benefit from un upgrade.
Woman	I thought they were acceptable, but I would have preferred a tent closer to the toilets. It was a bit of a trek during the night! For me, what stood out was how well organised they are. I mean, all the codes and information were on the app.
Man	And the fact that there was someone at reception 24 hours was fantastic. Not every campsite is like that, you know.

6. You hear two people talking about a concert. They agree that:

- **A** the sound quality was poor.
- **B** the venue was too crowded.
- **C** the band were disappointing.

Transcript

Woman	So, what did you think of the concert? It was so hot in there, wasn't it?!
Man	Yeah, I know! I was surprised, really. I mean, it can't have been from all the people considering the place was only half full.
Woman	Well, I can see why that was. I mean, the group was an hour late and only played a couple of their most well-known songs.

Part 1 | Answers

Man	Yeah, it's a real shame – especially since the ticket prices weren't cheap – and I couldn't hear anything other than the lead guitar!
Woman	Really? Maybe that's because you were standing in front of that massive speaker! You should have moved somewhere else.
Man	Oh, I hadn't even realised that might be why!

Part 1: Put it to the test 1 | Answers (pages 12–13)

1. You hear two parents talking about their children's football match. How does the woman feel about the match?

   A The final result was unfair.
   B One team played badly.
   C It was an exciting match.

Transcript

Woman	Well, I'm glad that's over.
Man	Me too. What a boring game! That second half was terrible. It was like most of the kids were just waiting for the final whistle to blow.
Woman	Probably because of the rain! That usually makes everyone lose a bit of motivation. Still, I don't think the other team deserved to win really.
Man	Why not? I thought they played pretty well.
Woman	Oh yes, I'm not saying that. I just think so did my son's team – and we had more chances – but that's life, I suppose.

2. You hear a news story on local radio. What is the purpose of the announcement?

   A To promote an event
   B To recommend an activity
   C To support a proposal

Transcript

And in local news, the mayor's office has just announced that the new leisure centre will be officially opened in May, just in time for summer. This will be welcome news for all parents out there who've suffered two summers without any swimming facilities in the town. As well as two pools, the leisure centre includes tennis courts and a number of pitches for football and other sports. The mayor herself will attend the opening, and there will be music from local bands and a chance for people to take a look around. Entry will be free all day for residents to go and see what they think.

B2 Listening | Cambridge Masterclass

3. You hear part of a conversation between a customer and a tourist office assistant. What does the woman want to know about?

- **A** Train times
- **B** Airport transfers
- **C** Bus tours

Transcript

Woman	Hi again! I hope you remember me!
Man	Yes, I do! How was the tour? I hope you enjoyed it!
Woman	I had a great time, but it rained a bit, so the open-top bus wasn't ideal. Thanks so much for your recommendation, though. In fact, I wondered if I could bother you again.
Man	Of course, what can I help you with?
Woman	Well, my flight home leaves tomorrow at 8am, and I wondered if it was best to take the train, bus or taxi?
Man	Hmmm. It's a tricky time, to be honest. The trains won't be running so early, but there's a shuttle bus that goes every hour on the hour – let me give you a leaflet.

4. You hear a station announcement about a delayed train. Passengers who want to go to Manchester should:

- **A** wait for information.
- **B** buy a new ticket.
- **C** take another train.

Transcript

This is an announcement for all passengers on platform 6 who are waiting for the ten forty-seven train to Manchester. Unfortunately, this train is delayed by approximately 45 minutes. This is due to the fact that it is currently behind a broken-down train on the same track. We will provide updates as soon as we have more information. However, at the moment we advise all passengers wanting to go to Manchester to board the next train on platform 6 and change at Birmingham. If you need to change your ticket, please go to the information desk and they will exchange it for you for no charge.

5. You hear two friends talking about booking tickets. They agree to:

- **A** wait until later.
- **B** get them in person.
- **C** sit separately.

Part 1 | Answers

Transcript

Woman	I keep refreshing the page, but I still can't find seats for us all together.
Man	Keep looking, though. I don't think we'll find anything better if we leave it any longer.
Woman	Do you think it might be better if we go down to the ticket office and ask?
Man	I don't think so. After all, surely their screens are showing the exact same thing as ours.
Woman	Hmmm. Maybe you're right.
Man	Look, I think we should just get what's available, even if we're in two different blocks. After all, we're there to hear the music!
Woman	Yes, you're right. I suppose there's no use waiting!

6. You hear a gardener talking about his work. What does he dislike about his job?

   A   The salary is quite low.
   B   The work is unpredictable.
   C   The schedule is exhausting.

Transcript

You know, I do feel extremely lucky because I get to spend my working days out in nature rather than sitting at a computer all day long – I can't imagine being stuck inside all day, to be honest. But don't get me wrong, there are some downsides as well. Sometimes we have to work long hours, especially in the spring when there's so much planting to be done, but the main issue is that it's seasonal work. I worry about the months when there's far less work, and it means I have to budget carefully throughout the year and make sure I save money for when work is more limited.

7. You hear two friends talking about online shopping. What annoys the man?

   A   Poor products
   B   Slow payment
   C   Delivery charges

Transcript

Woman	I picked up a great bargain online last night – a coffee table for only 50 pounds!
Man	Well, let's hope it's what you want.
Woman	What do you mean?

Man	Obviously it depends on the site, but I find lots of these things are not as good as they first appear.
Woman	Really?
Man	Yes. I bought some bedside tables that were basically full of scratches and dents – *and* it took about three weeks for them to arrive.
Woman	That's terrible, but I suppose I just find it far more convenient to shop online. Even dealing with a slow website is quicker than going to the shops.
Man	No doubt it's quicker, but you can sometimes pay for it in the end by choosing speed over quality.

8. You hear a teacher talking to her students. What is she telling them about?

A   Changes to exam dates.

B   Arrangements for a trip.

C   An important email.

Transcript

Okay everyone – sit down and pay attention. I need to give you some important information about the trip we're going on next week. Because it's after your final exams at the end of the month, we've decided you should get to choose where we go. Your parents will receive a message from the principal with all the options, and you'll need to reply with your first and second choices by Friday. Please remind your parents that they have to tick the box saying they agree. We need their permission, otherwise you won't be able to take part in the trip and I don't want that to happen to anyone.

Part 1: Put it to the test 2 | Answers   (pages 13–14)

1. You hear two people talking about an art exhibition. What do they agree about?

A   The artist was brilliant.

B   It needed more artworks.

C   The works were confusing.

Transcript

Woman	I can't believe the artist was at her own exhibition!
Man	Yes, it was brilliant! Great to get some idea of what was going through her head when she made the pieces.
Woman	Absolutely. Without that I would have been completely lost.

Part 1 | Answers

Man	You're not the only one! I think it's always a bit difficult to work out what is going on in an abstract piece.
Woman	Still, considering she's only been painting for seven years, she's done an impressive amount of paintings.
Man	Well, I thought there might have been some more to be honest, but I still really enjoyed what I saw. We should go to more things like this!

2. You hear two people talking about buying a new car. What is important for the woman?

   A Brand

   ☐ **B** Size

   C Cost

Transcript

Woman	I've been having real difficulties trying to find a new car.
Man	Well, they're pretty expensive nowadays, even the second-hand ones.
Woman	Yes, but that's not really the issue. I'd be happy to spend quite a lot, but finding something suitable is proving to be tricky.
Man	But I thought you were happy with your car?
Woman	Well, it used to be fine but now that I've got a dog I feel like I need something with more boot space. However, many of the ones I've looked at don't look like they would fit much in.
Man	Hmmm. That's a shame. Perhaps you should ask around to see if anyone has any suggestions for good car companies.

3. You hear a tour guide talking about a city. Why does he recommend the old town?

   ☐ **A** To hear traditional music.

   B To eat cheaply.

   C To see great architecture.

Transcript

If you've only got a few days in this city, make sure you go and see the old town. Well, we call it 'old' but actually a lot of it has been rebuilt over the years, so it isn't that great for fans of traditional architecture. However, the old town is absolutely THE place for seeing local people singing the tunes that have been the heart and soul of this city for hundreds of years. There are plenty of cafés and restaurants there, and they're very popular with tourists. Because of this, the prices aren't as reasonable as other areas in town, but the experience more than makes up for that.

B2 Listening | Cambridge Masterclass

4. You hear part of an interview with an actor. How did he get started in his career?

- **A** He met a director by chance.
- **B** He was hired by an agency.
- **C** He applied for a lot of roles.

Transcript

Woman	You've been in quite a few movies recently, but I'm sure people are keen to know how you got started.
Man	Okay. Well, my story is rather dull actually.
Woman	Oh, really? I thought perhaps you were spotted by a talent agent at acting school.
Man	No, nothing like that. For me it was just all hard work. After acting school, I spent three years trying to get acting job parts. It was quite depressing to get rejected a lot, but finally I got a small part in a movie that was a box office hit. I know lots of people have stories where they were working in a restaurant and served a director lunch one day, but not me.

5. You will hear a man leaving an answerphone message. What is the main reason for his message?

- **A** To promise something
- **B** To blame someone
- **C** To praise somewhere

Transcript

Hi there. It's John Sanders here, marketing director in head office. I'm just calling to talk about the work event we had last week at the Royston Centre. I'm not sure who booked it, but it was completely unsuitable for a company event. It's more like a community centre! That might be fine for some groups of people, but not for a world-leading manufacturer like us. Whoever it was who booked this needs to be spoken to, as far as I'm concerned. I mean, it's your department's job to get these kinds of things right. I'd also like you to guarantee that places are checked more carefully in the future. Thank you.

6. You hear two people talking about changes in their town. What does the woman think about the art gallery?

- **A** It is a positive addition to the town.
- **B** It will be welcomed by residents.
- **C** It has changed the look of the town.

Transcript

Woman	I visited the new art gallery in the town centre the other day, and I was really impressed. I mean, the design is not really to my taste but that's not the point. I think the gallery space works well and it'll attract tourists too.
Man	I'm not sure local people want even more tourists in the town centre, but I actually like the building. I think having something a bit more modern is a nice contrast to all the historical buildings there.
Woman	Well, I'm sure it'll be popular with the younger generation, especially the current exhibition all about the history of street art.

Check your answer by trying to rule out the other two options. You will have a second chance to listen to the extracts and check your answer.

7. You hear two people talking about a trip. What are they discussing?

   A   The transport
   B   The accommodation
   C   The day trips

Transcript

Man	Hmmm. I'm not sure we should stay in the middle of nowhere.
Woman	Why not? The city will be full of tourists out on trips, and I'd rather avoid the crowds.
Man	Yes, I understand that, but we only have one car and there's eight of us. It'll be impossible for us all to get there as there'll be no public transport that reaches that far out.
Woman	Hmmm… I suppose you have a point there. It's disappointing though.
Man	Maybe we can find a compromise and get somewhere in a village not too far away from the nearest bus, and we'd still be able to go on trips easily.
Woman	Okay, let's have a look on the web for more options.

8. You hear a student talking about finishing her university course. How does she feel about the experience?

   A   It made her more realistic.
   B   It was too competitive.
   C   It changed her work goals.

B2 Listening | Cambridge Masterclass

Transcript

I can't believe it's all over really. The course was very intense, and we all had to work extremely hard, but everyone was really supportive – it wasn't like some courses where the students are always trying to do better than each other. The assignments were tough, but they gave me real insight into the world of fashion design and I'm grateful for that. I think before, my understanding of the industry was too innocent, but at least now I know what to expect. Overall, I really enjoyed the course and I'd recommend it to anyone who is passionate about getting into fashion.

Part 2: Practise 1 | Answers   (page 16)

Nick was originally interested in being a (1)_____.

Noun – job: doctor, teacher, police officer?

While he was at university, Nick worked at a (2)_____.

Noun – place: restaurant, clothes shop, supermarket

Nick's (3)_____ were pleased that he decided to be a chef.

Noun – group of people (it must be plural because 'were' follows the space) – friends, parents, brothers, teachers

Doing a college course gave Nick some (4)_____ for cookery.

Noun – (plural because of 'some'): ideas, money, experience, enjoyment

Part 2: Practise 2 | Answers   (pages 16–17)

Nick was originally interested in being a (1) _Lawyer_.

While he was at university, Nick worked at a (2) _bike shop_.

Nick's (3) _housemates_ were pleased that he decided to be a chef.

Doing a college course gave Nick some (4) _(basic) skills_ for cookery.

42

Part 2 | Answers

Transcript (Part 1)

Hello. My name is Nick, and I'm going to tell you all about what it takes to be a chef. Now, I didn't always want to be a chef but I was always interested in food. You see, my dad is a farmer and I grew up helping out a lot. But actually, I wanted to be a lawyer. It sounded much more exciting! (1)

It all changed when I went to university, though, and I started cooking my own food. I found that more interesting than my degree course. I used to study during the day and then get cooking books out of the library to find out more about it. I did all that while helping out at a bike shop, and I spent everything that I made there on trying new foods. (2)

I decided at the end of my degree that I wanted to be a chef. It was a bit of a shock for my parents, who thought I had wasted my time at university, but my housemates were really supportive of me. But they had tasted the food I'd learnt to cook, and they knew I had talent. (3)

So, I started looking for training courses. I could have done another degree, but I wanted practical experience in a kitchen. I ended up doing a part-time course and also working as an apprentice chef part-time too. I picked up lots of basic skills on the course, like working with meat and how to store foods, and I learnt creativity and speed in the restaurant. (4)

Don't write too much. Answers will be no more than three words in length.

Part 2: Practise 3 | Answers (page 17)

Nick thinks that the (5) _____hours_____ is the hardest thing about being a chef.

At first, Nick couldn't add much (6) _____creativity_____ to his dishes.

Nick thinks the best dish on the menu is the (7) _(whole) salmon_.

Nick tries to avoid making (8) _____desserts_____ if he can.

The approach of (9) _sharing (food)_ makes Nick's restaurant different from others.

Nick recommends gaining some (10) _____experience_____ as a first step into being a chef.

B2 Listening | Cambridge Masterclass

Transcript (Part 2)

A lot of people say that the most difficult thing about being a chef is the pressure. The kitchen is a busy place – but for me that's exciting. The hours, though, are probably the most challenging part. I often miss family gatherings and normally I don't finish until midnight. (5)

I'm used to it now, however. And I wouldn't swap my job for anything. It's ten years since I trained, and now I work as a head chef. It's a brilliant position as I get to show my creativity, which was much harder to do when I started out. Then, my dishes needed to be exactly how someone else told me to do them. (6)

We've got plenty of dishes on the menu, and most of them I've come up with myself. Our most popular dish by far is the rib of beef, but my personal favourite is the whole salmon. It's the most expensive dish we serve, but it's absolutely worth it! We serve lots of fish dishes, actually. I developed a love of fish cookery when I was doing my training, as well as pasta-making, which I find really relaxing. I do, however, try to stay out of one section of the kitchen where possible – desserts aren't for me! Every chef has their limits, and my talents just aren't in that area! But thankfully I have some very talented chefs who can do desserts far better than me! (7) (8)

We've always wanted to be inventive in the restaurant, and I think we've achieved that. So many restaurants in this city are similar. We wanted to stand out, so we decided to make our restaurant all about sharing food. So, our dishes will feed two or three people. It's a great way to eat. (9)

Cooking is a really creative job, and I'd recommend it to anyone. Of course, you must have a love of food, but most of all you need dedication. If you think it's the job for you, try to get some experience in a restaurant first of all. That will give you a taste of the job, and then you'll know if you'd like to work towards some qualifications. (10)

Part 2: Put it to the test 1 I Answers   (page 18)

Grace thinks the best thing about the island is the **(1)**___*peace*___.

Visitors can often view different types of **(2)**___*sea birds*___ from the boat.

After some people going to **(3)**___*Iceland*___ stopped at the island, it became famous.

(4)___*(Tour) boats*___ are too large to get into the cave.

Its alternative name probably comes from a visit by a **(5)**___*composer*___.

Part 2 | Answers

The **(6)** _(stormy) winters_ caused the only people living on the island to leave.

The only building on the island is a **(7)** _shelter_.

The island is now owned by a **(8)** _charity_.

You can walk up to the **(9)** _highest point_ during the tours.

It's a good idea to look at the **(10)** _weather forecast_ before going on a tour.

Transcript

We've got lots of tours to the island of Staffa, and it's quite a special place to see. We often ask our visitors what they enjoyed most about it, and they usually say the nature. But personally I love the island for its peace. There's no one around for miles, and it just makes you feel so relaxed. You'll see what I mean if you go there! **(1)**

The *only* way to reach the island is via boat. It takes about an hour, and if you're lucky you'll get a view of the dolphins which occasionally swim in these waters. You're sure to see lots of sea birds there, though, and there is quite a variety of these. The boats usually have binoculars so you can get a closer look. **(2)**

Little is known about the island's early history, but for a while it became quite a popular tourist destination. It became more well-known after a visit from Englishman Joseph Banks and Daniel Solander, from Sweden. They were scientists who stopped at the island on their way to Iceland. As they were so impressed by the island they wrote about it, starting its steady stream of visitors. **(3)**

They were impressed by the nature of the island, but particularly a cave in the cliffs. This is really what made the island stand out for them. The cave is a sea cave, but while it's possible for walkers to get through the small entrance on foot there is a natural path along the bottom of the cliffs – it's too small for the tour boats, so, if the weather is nice, the best way to enter is to swim in – or you can always hire kayaks. **(4)**

This cave is called Fingal's Cave, but it's also known to some people as the Musical Cave. This is probably because it inspired composer Felix Mendelssohn to write a piece of music after visiting it. It's also been the inspiration for painters and writers too. The cave is unlike others in the area as it's formed of columns. It looks like something a human might build, but it's completely natural. **(5)**

Nobody lives on the island these days, but there is a record of a single family living there hundreds of years ago. It was probably a difficult life for them, and in the end they left the island. You'd think living there would have been too lonely, but actually it was the stormy winters that made life there simply too difficult. The farmhouse they lived in isn't there anymore. In fact, the only place still standing is a shelter used by travellers. **(6)** **(7)**

There aren't even toilets there! But don't worry: there are facilities on the boats!

Staffa Island was owned by a private individual for a long time, and then in 1986 it was given to a charity that works on preserving the area. This is great for visitors because it means the island is protected as well as all its wildlife. **(8)**

You definitely won't regret going on a tour of the island. It isn't that big, and there's a walking trail that you can do which takes around half an hour. You can pretty easily get up to the highest point and then see great views of the surrounding islands. Most boats stop if they can, so you will have a chance to explore. **(9)**

And that's one thing I need to mention about the tours. If the sea is rough, then the boats can't land on the island. So, make sure to check the weather forecast. Normally the tour leaders will let you know if there is a problem, but it's a good idea to check before you book too. **(10)**

Part 2: Put it to the test 2 | Answers (page 19)

The residents in Martin's block of flats wanted the garden to be used for **(1)** _relaxation_ .

Adding some **(2)** _flowers_ will make the community garden brighter and more attractive.

The residents **(3)** _share_ the various jobs that need doing in the garden.

Martin was surprised that he needed a lot of **(4)** _time_ to do the spraying.

The covered **(5)** _seating area_ means that people can be in the garden all year round.

Martin noticed that the residents **(6)** _behave_ differently because of the garden.

Community gardens in cities highlight the importance of **(7)** _nature_ and connection.

It is common to see gardens on **(8)** _office blocks_ and public buildings.

Martin points out that the roofs of city buildings are often **(9)** _empty_ .

Part 2 | Answers

The residents might invest in **(10)** _equipment_ so they can use rainwater in the garden.

Transcript

I live in a block of flats, and it has always had some grass all around it which no one really used. At a residents' meeting last year, we discussed what to do with it and there were various suggestions. But what most people said was they wanted a garden – not for growing vegetables or having barbecues, but as a quiet space for relaxation for all the residents. (1)

So, this spring we got started. We planted some bushes and some small fruit trees that grow quickly to give some shade for the summer. At the moment the garden is a bit dull, and we want to encourage more people to enjoy it all year round. This means we'll need to plant a lot more flowers and find out what will bring colour in different seasons. (2)

If people are interested in gardening, they can help grow the plants, but they don't have to. What we do ask is that residents volunteer for all the necessary tasks. Things like watering the plants, checking for insects, cutting back the trees and so on. We decided to share all the work rather than paying a gardener to do it. The garden is quite large, and the residents would prefer to spend their money on flowers and trees and equipment instead. It's a lot of work, though. We made a list of all the tasks to do over the year to help us get organised. I volunteered to spray the plants – I couldn't believe how much time it took! Next time I think I'll ask for some help! (3) (4)

So far, I think everyone is delighted with what we've done. On sunny days the whole neighbourhood is outside enjoying the space or working to improve it. But actually, even when the weather isn't so great residents use the garden. We built a seating area with a roof on top and some people even come out in the rain and snow! (5)

Another benefit that the garden has brought is that people are getting to know each other better. I've been observing how people behave in the garden, and everyone is much more chatty now. I found out that one of my neighbours was born in the same part of the country as me and another loves hiking like I do. We're arranging a trip together for next month! Benefits like these have made community gardens quite common in cities nowadays. The idea is to bring a little bit of the countryside into our urban spaces and make us feel healthier. These gardens brighten up city environments. They remind us that we should spend time in nature and increase communication with the people around us. (6) (7)

And, of course, they're good for the environment too. You might have seen a few on top of office blocks, as well as on other large buildings like museums, hospitals and libraries. All the extra plants improve the air quality in cities, and they provide habitats for birds and insects like bees. I don't understand why more buildings don't have them. (8)

There are so many empty roofs, and all that space could be used for community gardens. I mean, they're not being used for anything else, so it seems like such a waste. (9)

What I especially like about many rooftop gardens is the chance to collect rainwater rather than letting it disappear down the pipes. ==We are thinking of trying to do this in our garden, but not on the roof of the block of flats. There's a lot of equipment you can buy that collects rainwater on the ground.== Our aim is to recycle it back into the garden so we don't have use water from the flats. We have lots of future plans for our garden! **(10)**

Part 3: Practise 1 | Answers   (page 22)

The question focuses on the main goal of practising sport.

A to train with other people more

        train = play, practise / **other people** = other players, competitors

B to increase their physical strength

        increase = improve, raise, get better / **physical strength** = muscles, body, strong, powerful

C to become more sociable

        more sociable = friendly, go out more, attend events, meet more people

D to strengthen their determination

        strengthen = improve, build up, increase / **determination** = motivation

E to implement a routine

        implement = put in place, have, get, develop / **routine** = schedule, timetable, habits

F to win a competition

        win = come first, be the best / **competition** = game, race, match, tournament

G to improve a specific technique

        improve = increase, get better, develop / **specific technique** = method, approach, skill

H to manage stress from work

        manage = cope with, face, deal with
        stress = stressful situations, problems
        work = in my job, at the office

Part 3: Practise 2 | Answers (pages 22–23)

A to train with other people more
B to increase their physical strength
C to become more sociable
D to strengthen their determination
E to implement a routine
F to win a competition
G to improve a specific technique
H to manage stress from work

Speaker 1: **1 B**
Speaker 2: **2 E**

Speaker 1

I'm training for a marathon next year. I don't think it will be too difficult because I've run some 10K races before. I'm quite self-motivated and have created my own schedule: I run three times a week before work and then once at the weekend with my running club. But the thing I'm a little bit concerned about is whether I'm strong enough. I'm going to need to spend a lot more time in the gym doing weights and exercises to build up my leg muscles. At the moment they're good for short distances, but I have to change this if I want to actually finish a marathon.

Speaker 2

I took up yoga last year because I work long hours at a computer and was suffering from hip pain. At first, I found it hard to build time for yoga into my daily life. I was always distracted by something. I decided to join a class, which gave me some structure, and the classes started to make a difference – and now I feel more motivated to do it at home. I aim to plan my home yoga sessions at the beginning of each week and make sure that nothing gets in the way. I've got quite a busy and stressful life, but I'm sure I can devote time to it.

B2 Listening | Cambridge Masterclass

Part 3: Practise 3 | Answers   (page 23)

A	to train with other people more	Speaker 3: **3 D**
B	to increase their physical strength	Speaker 4: **4 C**
C	to become more sociable	Speaker 5: **5 G**
D	to strengthen their determination	
E	to implement a routine	
F	to win a competition	
G	to improve a specific technique	
H	to manage stress from work	

Speaker 3

I'm quite a sporty person, so when one of my work colleagues suggested we play golf together I thought it was a great idea. The only problem is that I'm a terrible golfer, even after having had lessons for a few months. But I'm not going to give up like I did with tennis last year. I know it'll take time to improve, and I just have to work at it. My golf coach used to be a professional player, and she says I just have to stay positive whenever I make mistakes. I love the community spirit of the place, though. There's a great atmosphere, and I've met so many nice people at the different events they have.

Speaker 4

Recently, I noticed that I haven't been as involved in my badminton club as lots of the other members. I usually just chat with a couple of friends who I play games with. Anyway, I've decided to attend the club dinners that are held at the end of each month after the club competitions. I'd like to get know everyone more, even if I am a bit shy. I think it'd be good for my game too – you know, talking about techniques and different types of shots. I don't really know which aspects of my game I should work on, so it might have an extra benefit if I learn something too.

Speaker 5

My swimming club is a really social place. I love taking part in the competitions that they organise. I've been improving my strength a lot recently by training more regularly. I also got a coach to identify areas for improvement. My diving is the issue, though, and I should try not to splash as much. My coach has videoed me so that he can explain what I'm doing wrong. I didn't think I was that motivated to improve, but the more I train the more this is starting to change. I'm becoming more competitive as I get better.

Part 3: Put it to the test 1 | Answers (page 24)

A Thinks it's too complicated
B Enjoys the sense of adventure
C Makes them feel nervous
D Prefers flying alone
E Finds it uncomfortable
F Likes the service
G Enjoys the luxury
H Likes looking out the window

Speaker 1: **1 E**
Speaker 2: **2 F**
Speaker 3: **3 A**
Speaker 4: **4 H**
Speaker 5: **5 D**

Speaker 1

I never particularly enjoyed flying when I was younger. I was a bit afraid of it, to be honest, but now I don't mind it at all. I mean, it's a quick way to travel. Of course, at one metre ninety tall, the seats aren't perfect for me, and I suppose that's my major problem with it, but I try to get up and move about the cabin as much as I can, and I never choose a window seat as I think they're the worst for someone like me! When I'm travelling for work, though, they fly me business class, which is much better – in all areas.

Speaker 2

I'm used to flying. My parents always took me on overseas holidays, and now I fly almost every week for work. It's never much of an adventure, though, as I always go back and forth to the same place: London to New York! I get quite bored sometimes, just staring out at the same old view of the Atlantic, but I've got to say the cabin staff are excellent, and nothing is too much trouble for them. Although, I think they probably know me by now, as I always fly from the same airports and on the same airline! Of course, I'd prefer to fly less, especially because of the environment, but I need to do it for my job.

Speaker 3

The thought of flying away to some amazing destination on holiday is always exciting, but I don't think the reality is quite the same. Normally, the travelling part of the holiday is far from a luxury. The size of the airports, having to go through security checks, endless queueing to get on the plane and trying to find your gate in time – it gets on my nerves! I miss those simple days of just getting in the car and heading to the coast. That's what I used to do with my parents. And we'd look out onto the countryside, singing songs. Those were the days!

Speaker 4

I don't understand people who worry about flying. After all, it's one of the safest forms of travel. I certainly find it an enjoyable way to get from A to B. It used to be a real experience, with great service and everything. I don't think it's quite the same these days, but there's nothing better than watching the clouds pass you by or spotting a mountain or city far below. I suppose, when I think of it, it's my favourite way to travel. I kind of feel like the airplane is my safe place. I'm often more worried about what's going to happen at the other end, like if I can't get to my hotel from the airport or something. Then, the adventure really begins!

Speaker 5

I suppose I don't mind flying, but I don't particularly enjoy it either. You see, I get quite easily bored on a plane, especially on a longer flight. After all, there's not particularly anywhere to go or anything to do. Add onto that the time it takes to get through security and passport control, and it can seem like forever. Although, I must say, it's much worse when I fly with others, especially the kids. It's far more stressful for me even though they think it's a great adventure! Once they made so much noise, I felt completely uncomfortable for the whole flight.

Part 3: Put it to the test 2 | Answers   (page 24)

A   The worry of being a new student
B   The assistance from the staff
C   The design of the building
D   The excitement of making friends
E   The personality of their teacher
F   The equipment in their classroom
G   The number of people
H   The range of fun activities

Speaker 1: **1 F**
Speaker 2: **2 H**
Speaker 3: **3 B**
Speaker 4: **4 D**
Speaker 5: **5 G**

Speaker 1

I think it was enjoyable overall due to the amount of new and interesting experiences we had on that day. I made some new friends, I met a lot of adults who weren't like my parents and I got to play in an enormous playground. But I think what particularly stood out was seeing everything there was to help us learn. The teacher showed us the cupboards where all the pens and paints and books and calculators were kept. It was like being in a cave full of treasure! To be honest, a lot of my other memories have faded and I wish I was able to remember more about my teacher and my classmates.

Speaker 2

The school I went to as a child was completely new, so everyone in the area was really excited about seeing it for the first time. The facilities were modern, and there was a computer room too. It had that smell that all new buildings have. We did so many things – games, painting, singing and running around in the playground – and I thought it was all amazing. A few of the other children in my class started crying when their parents left, but not me! I don't really remember much about my teacher on that day. Probably because there were so many different teachers and we met lots of other staff members too.

Speaker 3

My parents were quite nervous about me starting school because I was shy when I was younger. But they shouldn't have worried at all because the staff were always checking if the students were okay. I can clearly remember that I got lost on my way to the toilet because the building was so enormous. Anyway, one of the cleaning staff found me and showed me where to go, which I was really relieved about. I told my parents about it, which I think made them more relaxed because they saw that it wasn't just the teachers who were kind and that everyone there wanted to look after us.

Speaker 4

In the weeks leading up to the beginning of term, I kept asking my parents so many questions about school. Would my teacher be friendly, how many kids would be in my class, how big was the school, and so on. As an only child, the idea of school was really appealing to me. I couldn't wait to meet my classmates and find out what they were like. And I was not disappointed! The other children were super friendly, and we all got on well together – well, most of the time. Except when we thought someone had taken our calculator or tablet or something like that.

Speaker 5

The staff were probably exhausted by the end of that first day since quite a lot of children seemed to be nervous and wouldn't let go of their parents. I'd never seen that many children in one building before! Everywhere you looked, children were running around, shouting and screaming with either excitement or fear. Although I'll never forget it, I wasn't concerned about it though – coming from a large family, I'm used to noise. I don't recall much about the classroom activities, but we might have played some games. You know, I'm still friends with a couple of people I met on that first day all these years later.

B2 Listening | Cambridge Masterclass

Part 4: Practise 1 | Answers   (page 26)

1. Alex believes summer camps are a <u>good experience</u> because:
2. How are summer camps <u>different from school</u>?
3. What does Alex say <u>teenagers develop</u> on the camp?

- A Things that teenagers learn on summer camps ✓
- B A description of different types of summer camp ☐
- C Why teenagers prefer summer camps to school ☐
- D How to help teenagers who get homesick ☐
- E A comparison with school activities ✓
- F Advantages of attending a summer camp ✓

Part 4: Practise 2 | Answers   (pages 26–27)

1. Alex believes summer camps are a good experience because:

   - A they only last a short time.
   - B the staff are well qualified.
   - **C there is a range of activities on offer.**

2. How are summer camps different from school?

   - A They have more activities.
   - **B They are more flexible.**
   - C They focus more on skills.

3. What does Alex say teenagers develop on the camp?

   - A Leadership skills
   - B Independence
   - **C Self confidence**

Extract 1

Interviewer I'm joined this morning by Alex Blakely, manager of the UK's largest summer camp. He believes that all parents should seriously consider sending their teenagers on a summer camp. So, tell us Alex, why are you convinced that this is such as great idea?

Part 4 | Answers

Alex	Hello. Well, for me it's about opening their eyes to new things. In their daily lives, teenagers might go to a dance class or play a sport or attend a weekly group like Scouts. But here they're able to try out so many things they've never done before. Our staff have a lot of experience working with young people, and we really want them to make the most of their time with us. After all, most participants only spend two or three weeks at camp.
Interviewer	Some parents don't want to pay for an experience that they feel is similar to school. What is your opinion on this?
Alex	Even though the teenagers are a similar age, and the activities are all learning experiences, summer camps are unique. This is because there is a lot more freedom. We don't have a prescribed programme. Also, we encourage participants to get involved with as many or as few activities as they want.
Interviewer	What skills do teenagers learn at the camp?
Alex	At this age, young people are developing their identity quite rapidly. We're keen to show them ways to do this successfully. Although they cannot be fully in charge of their day-to-day lives, we want them to grow as people. Positive learning experiences at the camp make students see their abilities more clearly.

1 C

2 B

3 C

Part 4: Practise 3 | Answers (pages 27–28)

4. What do the camp counsellors help teenagers do?

   A   solve friendship issues.
   B   be more emotional.
   C   learn how to argue.

5. Why are teenagers not allowed mobile phones at the camp?

   A   to help them rely on technology less.
   B   to prevent contact with their parents.
   C   to improve communication skills.

6. When choosing a summer camp, parents prefer places that:

   A   are convenient to get to.
   B   offer water sports.
   C   other parents recommend.

Watch out for **distractors** – information that may lead to choosing a wrong answer!

7. After summer camp, parents often report that their children:

- **A** keep the house tidier.
- **B** get up earlier in the morning.
- **C** organise themselves better.

Extract 2

Interviewer — What about teenagers who are nervous about attending a summer camp?

Man — Some parents worry about this. Remember that the staff are trained in techniques for communicating with young people. Everyone has a personal counsellor who helps smooth over any disagreements. We resolve all conflicts as they happen to show how to build relationships but also how to manage conflict. Part of the experience we offer is the opportunity to communicate with adults who are not parents or teachers. **4 | A**

Interviewer — Do you allow the use of mobile phones on the camp?

Man — That's an excellent question and one we get asked all the time. We state very clearly that teenagers have to leave their mobile phones at home. This is not because we don't want them using technology – we have tablets and laptops for our creative activities. The reason is that we don't want them calling home all the time because parents tend to worry. Also, they've come to the camp to make friends and have fun outside, not spend all day on social media. **5 | B**

Interviewer — Talking of nature, how important is the location of summer camps in general?

Man — Most of them are chosen because they are near rivers or lakes so that water sports can be included on the programme. This is one of the biggest attractions for most camps. But parents are usually thinking about the drive! If they're too remote, or the journey is complicated, parents are likely to think twice because of the inconvenience. So that is always considered when choosing venues. **6 | A**

Interviewer — And finally, in your experience, what changes do parents notice most when their children return from camp?

Man — Um, I think what they see immediately is how their children have become better able to care for themselves in general. Camp teaches them to get themselves together in the mornings. We expect them to be on time for activities and bring everything they need. Some parents also say their children are more willing to help around the house, perhaps helping with dinner or cleaning the car. **7 | C**

Interviewer — These are all good benefits! Okay, well that's all we have time for. Thank you, Alex.

Part 4: Put it to the test 1 | Answers (pages 28–29)

1. What does Victoria say about studying to be a vet?

   A It was harder than she expected.
   B She adapted to the course demands.
   C It was a rewarding experience.

2. According to Victoria, team meetings help the vets:

   A deal with stressful situations.
   B make decisions more quickly.
   C come up with new approaches.

3. Why is talking to pet owners difficult for vets?

   A They are very emotional.
   B They can be unpredictable.
   C They want positive news.

4. Working as a farm vet helped Victoria to:

   A rely on her knowledge.
   B improve her communication.
   C manage her schedule.

5. What did Victoria admire about farmers?

   A Their approach to animals' health issues.
   B The way they communicate with vets.
   C How they care for their animals.

6. Victoria thinks that managing a veterinary practice:

   A is something she would like to do one day.
   B could become boring after a while.
   C would not be the best use of her skills.

7. How has technology affected Victoria's job?

   A The paperwork has been reduced.
   B The practice has more customers.
   C The staff have become more efficient.

Extract 1

Interviewer Working as a vet is a childhood dream for many people. However, it takes many years of study and hard work. Today, I'm speaking to Victoria Bradshaw about the challenges and rewards of this demanding job. Firstly, Victoria, did you enjoying studying veterinary science at university?

Woman I must admit that at times I wondered if I'd done the right thing. The course is long and there is so much to learn. However, after my first year I noticed that it became easier. Or perhaps I just got tougher and more able to deal with the workload. I'm glad I stuck it out because I really enjoy my job. Every day I get to feel good, so it's very rewarding. **1 B**

Interviewer Can you tell us a little bit about your day-to-day work?

Woman Of course. We start at about 8.00 am with a team meeting to review all the animals that are being treated. Getting together means that we can benefit from talking through different treatments. Often this leads to fresh ideas about what to do or why a different medicine might work better. These meetings are vital for building confidence and sharing ideas. **2 C**

Interviewer What other skills do you need besides medical skills?

Woman We need to be able to communicate well. Most of the animals we see are pets, so there's a lot of talking to owners. Vets new to the job often find this upsetting. You never really know how someone is going to react to news, even when it's positive. But you have to get used to it and find a way to deal with it if you want to work as a vet. **3 B**

Interviewer Have you always worked with pets?

Woman Actually, I started out as a farm vet. The structure of that job is very different. You spend most of the time out and about on farm visits. And you spend a lot of time alone and don't have the chance to discuss things with your colleagues. But for me it was an excellent way to become more confident in my abilities. I had to get on with it and trust my instincts. **4 A**

Interviewer Did you enjoy working with farm animals and farmers?

Woman Yes, I did. During my training I became interested in the challenges of treating large animals. But soon I realised that a large part of the job is talking to farmers. You have to work hard to earn their trust because they already know so much about caring for and treating their own animals. I think this was why it was hard for me to communicate with pet owners at first. Because I'd spent so long with farmers who are much more practical about sickness and disease, I wasn't used to the emotional element required to work as a city vet. **5 A**

Interviewer Yes, I see. Would you like to have your own veterinary practice one day?

Woman It's something I have thought about, but I think my skills are more suited to animal care rather than people-management. I'm good at paperwork and keeping accurate records, but I'm less interested in hiring and training staff. And, of course, getting the right staff and keeping a team together is one of the most important parts of running a veterinary practice. **6 C**

Interviewer And has your job changed much in recent years?

Woman I think for me it's the amount we use technology, but not just for our medical work. Video calls, emails with photos and messaging on mobile phones means that we now provide services to more people, not just those who live nearby. It's transformed the practice and how we work compared to a decade ago…

Part 4: Put it to the test 2 | Answers   (pages 29–30)

1. Tom started playing chess because:

   A he liked intellectual games.
   B he wanted to please his parents.
   C he had friends in a local club.

2. The thing that most interests Tom about chess is that:

   A it involves a lot of luck.
   B there are many strategies.
   C each game is unique.

3. What do chess players begin to understand as they improve their skills?

   A That it is more difficult than it appears
   B That the rules are complicated
   C That losing is good for learning

4. What are the benefits of playing chess for the brain?

   A Improved intelligence
   B Better overall function
   C More creative thinking

5. What does Tom say about chess books?

   A They help beginners get started.
   B They are not worth the money.
   C They are useful for advanced players.

6. Tom thinks that chess remains popular because:

   A people of different ages like playing it.
   B there are so many opportunities to play it.
   C it is part of many cultures around the world.

7. What is Tom's assessment of playing chess against a computer?

   A   It prepares players for competitions.
   B   It provides limited practice.
   C   It gives a wide range of practice.

Extract 1

Interviewer   With me today is Tom Lawrence, who has recently written a book called *The Excitement of Chess*. Tom, you've been playing chess as a hobby and in national competitions for many years. What got you into it?

Man   When I was a teenager, my parents were worried that I didn't have any non-academic interests. They kept trying to get me interested in sport or music. For me, though, strategy games that involve puzzles and working things out were more exciting than physical ones. One day, when I was looking around a second-hand shop, I saw a chess board and decided to buy it. I started to play with my best friend, and we both loved it. We joined a local club and I've never looked back.   **1 | A**

Interviewer   That's a great story. Now, I'm sure not all our listeners would say that it's an exciting game so why do you think it is?

Man   I suppose it's the fact that every game is totally different. Even though players are using the same strategies and techniques, no two games are the same. I'm really intrigued by that idea, and I get a little rush of excitement every time the first piece is played in a game. Although, of course, like all strategy games, there is an element of luck too, which adds to the fun.   **2 | C**

Interviewer   Does it take a long time to become a good player?

Man   You know, one of the beauties of the game is that it never gets boring. Although it is easy to learn, they say it takes a lifetime to master chess. This is probably due to the fact that the more you play and lose, the more you want to improve. As you get more involved and learn new tricks, you start to see how complex it can really be.   **3 | A**

Interviewer   And what about people who are thinking of getting into chess for the intellectual factor? What would you say to them?

Man   Oh, I'd definitely encourage them to take up chess for that reason. There is overwhelming evidence that playing chess is good for the brain. Apparently, you use both sides of the brain when you play, which boosts your brain activity in all sorts of ways. Studies have shown that chess players remember more, their minds are sharper and they can focus better. I don't know if that makes them more intelligent though!   **4 | B**

Interviewer   Would you recommend that people have lessons or just give it a go?

Man   Well, first of all, let me say that there are no barriers to entry in chess. Buying a board is cheap, and you don't need any expensive equipment or lessons to begin playing. Most people just practise and learn new tactics and strategies that way. I mean, there are thousands of books you could

Part 4 | Answers

Man	buy to study the game, but it's not necessary. Perhaps, if you really get into it, you might consider buying a book to learn some of the classic moves by the grand masters.
Interviewer	Ah. Okay. And why do you think chess is still so popular?
Man	Well, it's been around for so long, which means it's spread all over the world. And now it can be played online as well, which means it's a game that can bring people together in the virtual world as well as the real world.
Interviewer	And finally, what are your thoughts on playing chess against a computer?
Man	Hmm. That's an interesting question! I would recommend it because all practice is good, but there are a couple of things to bear in mind. One is that computers are always logical when they play whereas humans are less predictable. I think you should practise with unexpected situations, too, and not just against computers, especially if you want to play in competitions.

5 C

6 B

7 B

Practice tests

Test 1 | pages 65–71

Part 1   *66*
Part 2   *68*
Part 3   *69*
Part 4   *70*

Test 2 | pages 73–79

Part 1   *74*
Part 2   *76*
Part 3   *77*
Part 4   *78*

Test 3 | pages 81–87

Part 1   *82*
Part 2   *84*
Part 3   *85*
Part 4   *86*

Test 4 | pages 89–95

Part 1   *90*
Part 2   *92*
Part 3   *93*
Part 4   *94*

Cambridge B2 First Listening

Practice test 1

 P_1_1

Part 1

You will hear people talking in eight different situations. For Questions 1–8, choose the correct answer, A, B or C.

1. You hear a teacher talking to a parent about their daughter's behaviour. What negative point does the teacher mention?

   A   She doesn't listen to instructions.
   B   She distracts other children.
   C   She doesn't work well in groups.

2. You hear two friends talking about a hotel they stayed at recently. What did they both enjoy about it?

   A   the range of food and drinks
   B   the location of the hotel
   C   the service from the staff

3. You hear a man talking about his hobby of growing tomatoes. What is he talking about?

   A   caring for the plants
   B   when to plant the seeds
   C   good soil for tomatoes

4. You hear a woman talking about wind farms. She thinks that the local government should:

   A   stop building them near houses.
   B   replace them with solar power.
   C   spend less money on them.

Transcripts on pages 96–98

Practice test 1

5. You hear a shop assistant talking to a customer.
   What is the man's opinion of the jacket?

   A   It's not his style.
   B   It's over his budget.
   C   It's the wrong colour.

6. You hear part of a news programme on the radio.
   Where will the new shopping centre be built?

   A   behind the train station
   B   on the edge of the town
   C   next to the business district

7. You hear two friends talking about getting fit.
   The woman is optimistic that she will:

   A   lose weight.
   B   become stronger.
   C   run faster.

8. You hear two friends talking about being members of a book club.
   Why did he join the book club?

   A   to get inspiration
   B   to discuss books
   C   to meet new people

Answers on pages 120–122

B2 Listening | Cambridge Masterclass

 P_1_2

Part 2

You will hear a tour guide talking about London Bridge to some visitors. For questions 9–18, complete the sentences with a word or short phrase.

___

Britain sold London Bridge because of problems with the **(9)**_____.

The previous bridge was too **(10)**_____ and had to be replaced.

The move of the bridge was completed in the **(11)**_____.

McCulloch's aim was for **(12)**_____ to buy property in the area.

Now, the inside of the bridge is made of **(13)**_____.

The bridge was initially rebuilt over **(14)**_____ when it came to Arizona.

The lights on the bridge change for **(15)**_____.

There are more **(16)**_____ than any other animal living on the bridge.

The **(17)**_____ mean that the bridge will last for many years.

The tour guide recommends the **(18)**_____ after the tour.

Transcripts on pages 98–100

Practice test 1

 P_1_3

Part 3

You will hear five short extracts in which people are talking about moving from the city to the countryside. For questions 19–23, choose from the list (A–H) what each person feels about it. Use the letters only once. There are three extra letters which you do not need to use.

A   It can be inconvenient.

B   There is a sense of community.

C   Entertainment could be improved.

D   Public transport is terrible.

E   Local shopkeepers are friendly.

F   The cost of living is lower.

G   More businesses are needed.

H   The quality of life is good.

Speaker 1:   19

Speaker 2:   20

Speaker 3:   21

Speaker 4:   22

Speaker 5:   23

Answers on pages 120–122

B2 Listening | Cambridge Masterclass

P_1_4

Part 4

You will hear part of a radio interview with Emily Jones, who is talking about the natural skincare products she makes. For Questions 24–30, choose the best answer (A, B or C).

---

24. Emily started making her own skincare products because:

   A she was interested in plants.
   B she needed to increase her income.
   C her son had skin problems.

25. What was difficult for Emily when she started her business?

   A marketing her products
   B finding time for research
   C getting customer feedback

26. Where did Emily find help to grow her business?

   A her previous manager
   B an online forum
   C a local business group

27. What does Emily enjoy about her job?

   A completing legal documents
   B responding to customer complaints
   C writing product descriptions

Transcripts on pages 100–101

70

28. Emily would advise small business owners to:

- **A** find a good accountant.
- **B** ask friends and family for help.
- **C** pay for a professional website.

29. According to Emily, people buy her products because they:

- **A** are good value for money.
- **B** are based on science.
- **C** use fewer chemicals.

30. Emily thinks that future skincare products will:

- **A** use sustainable packaging.
- **B** contain a lot of vitamins.
- **C** use organic ingredients.

Cambridge B2 First Listening

Practice test 2

B2 Listening | Cambridge Masterclass

 P_2_1

Part 1

You will hear people talking in eight different situations. For Questions 1–8, choose the correct answer, A, B or C.

---

1. You hear part of a conversation between two colleagues. What are they talking about?

   A a conference
   B a training course
   C a presentation

2. You hear an announcement at a sports match. What should families do?

   A wait to leave the stadium
   B ask for assistance
   C go out the West exit

3. You hear part of a conversation between a shop assistant and a customer. What is the problem with the phone?

   A it's got a poor battery
   B the screen is dark
   C it gets too hot

4. You hear two friends talking about their recent holiday. They agree that the:

   A resort was unpleasant.
   B weather was changeable.
   C hotel was disappointing.

Transcripts on pages 102–104

5. You hear a woman talking about a film she saw. Why did she watch the film?

   A   because she'd read about it
   B   because someone recommended it
   C   because she's a fan of the director

6. You hear a policeman talking about his job. What does he think about his job?

   A   It's harder than he thought.
   B   It's different to what people think.
   C   It's more boring than he expected.

7. You hear a woman talking about driving. What annoys the woman?

   A   slow drivers
   B   strong headlights
   C   bad parking

8. You hear an advertisement on the radio. What is it for?

   A   a hair salon
   B   a wedding planner
   C   a cleaning service

Answers on pages 120–122

B2 Listening | Cambridge Masterclass

 P_2_2

Part 2

You will hear a man called Hugo talking to a group of local people about road safety. For questions 9–18, complete the sentences with a word or short phrase.

The talk is focused on the safety of **(9)**_____.

Hugo will use information from some **(10)**_____ in the talk.

Failure to use a **(11)**_____ makes accidents more likely to occur.

People should wait to establish **(12)**_____ before walking across a road.

(13)_____ is recommended for people walking in the evenings.

Most accidents are caused by **(14)**_____.

The council has begun **(15)**_____ to improve the safety of walkers.

Hugo believes flashing road signs will be **(16)**_____.

The **(17)**_____ is a new road-safety technology we can use now.

The **(18)**_____ is keen on the development of artificial intelligence (AI) technologies.

Transcripts on pages 104–106

Practice test 2

 P_2_3

Part 3

You will hear five short extracts in which people are talking about an art course. For questions 19–23, choose from the list (A–H) why they decided to take the course. Use the letters only once. There are three extra letters which you do not need to use.

A   To help them relax.

B   To improve their ability.

C   To start a hobby.

D   To meet new people.

E   To complete a project.

F   To improve their opportunities.

G   To try something different.

H   To give them more confidence.

Speaker 1: 19
Speaker 2: 20
Speaker 3: 21
Speaker 4: 22
Speaker 5: 23

Answers on pages 120–122

Part 4

You will hear part of an interview with Chris Walker and Louise Franklin talking about what it's like to work as rock-climbing instructors. For Questions 24–30, choose the best answer (A, B or C).

---

24. Louise became interested in rock climbing after:

   A watching a documentary.
   B reading a book.
   C talking to a friend.

25. What made Chris and Louise decide to become instructors?

   A a bad experience on a course
   B joining a climbing club
   C watching other instructors

26. In order to become an instructor, it is necessary to:

   A have experience.
   B complete six courses.
   C pass an exam.

27. The instructor course highlighted that Chris needed to:

   A work on his physical condition.
   B improve his communication skills.
   C listen to instructions carefully.

Transcripts on pages 106–107

28. According to Louise, rock climbing is:

- **A** accessible to everyone.
- **B** a good personal challenge.
- **C** not as difficult as it looks.

29. What should people new to rock climbing bear in mind?

- **A** Don't be afraid of falling.
- **B** Don't give up too quickly.
- **C** Don't pay a lot for a course.

30. How has rock climbing affected Chris?

- **A** He is more connected to nature.
- **B** He has increased his self-confidence.
- **C** He feels more satisfied with life.

Answers on pages 120–122

Cambridge B2 First Listening

Practice test 3

B2 Listening | Cambridge Masterclass

P_3_1

Part 1

You will hear people talking in eight different situations. For Questions 1–8, choose the correct answer, A, B or C.

---

1. You hear an answerphone message. Why is the woman calling?

    A   to ask for some advice
    B   to change some plans
    C   to give some information

2. You hear part of a conversation about buying a house. Why does the man want a house with a garden?

    A   so his children can play outside.
    B   because he enjoys barbecues.
    C   so his dog has space to run around.

3. You hear a tour guide talking to a group of tourists. When was the original castle built?

    A   17th Century
    B   18th Century
    C   19th Century

4. You hear two friends making travel plans. Wgat does the man **not** want to do?

    A   get up early
    B   go by bus
    C   pay for a seat

Transcripts on pages 108–109

Practice test 3

5. You hear two friends talking about their work. What are they talking about?

   A a presentation
   B a project
   C an event

6. You hear two parents discussing dinner.
   What do they decide to do on Saturday night?

   A get a delivery
   B go to a restaurant
   C cook at home

7. You hear two friends arranging a day out together. What do they agree to go to?

   A a flower show
   B a play
   C a festival

8. You hear a teacher talking about mobile phones in the classroom.
   What does he think about them?

   A They should not be allowed in class.
   B They stop students concentrating.
   C They are a useful tool for teachers.

Answers on pages 120–122

B2 Listening | Cambridge Masterclass

 P_3_2

Part 2

You will hear a woman called Paula talking about developing video games. For questions 9–18, complete the sentences with a word or short phrase.

Most people play video games to gain a feeling of **(9)**_____.

One advantage of gaming is that it's an escape from **(10)**_____.

Paula works in the **(11)**_____.

The way the game looks often depends on what the **(12)**_____ is like.

Management gives the team a **(13)**_____ and deadline.

Paula describes the process of development as a **(14)**_____.

Most of their advertising is done through **(15)**_____.

They offer support in many different **(16)**_____.

They normally find a few **(17)**_____ after the game has been released.

Some people in the video game industry are **(18)**_____.

Transcripts on pages 110–112

Practice test 3

 P_3_3

Part 3

You will hear five short extracts in which people are talking about working with children. For questions 19–23, choose from the list (A–H) what each person enjoys about it. Use the letters only once. There are three extra letters which you do not need to use.

A   Seeing their personalities develop.

B   Learning about child psychology.

C   Seeing how creative they can be.

D   Discovering what they like to do.

E   Helping them solve problems.

F   Telling parents about their progress.

G   Researching new teaching techniques.

H   Watching them become more confident.

Speaker 1: [19]
Speaker 2: [20]
Speaker 3: [21]
Speaker 4: [22]
Speaker 5: [23]

Answers on pages 120–122

B2 Listening | Cambridge Masterclass

P_3_4

Part 4

You will hear a radio interview with a woman called Natasha Evans talking about what it's like to be the manager of a sports shop. For Questions 24–30, choose the best answer (A, B or C).

---

24. What does Natasha say is an important part of her job?

   A finding interesting new products
   B keeping up to date with sports news
   C watching different types of sports

25. What are young people most interested in buying?

   A designer trainers
   B football shirts
   C famous brands

26. According to Natasha, her success is a result of:

   A spending time with customers.
   B offering a range of products.
   C giving good discounts.

27. What aspect of the clothing and sportswear business is Natasha currently studying?

   A sustainable fashion
   B consumer behaviour
   C factory working conditions

Transcripts on pages 112–113

28. Natasha encourages her employees to:

   A   contribute their ideas.
   B   get more qualifications.
   C   attend industry events.

29. Natasha admits that she isn't always good at:

   A   using technology at work.
   B   having enough items in stock.
   C   preparing for surprises.

30. What does Natasha say is happening in her industry?

   A   attitudes to casual clothing are changing
   B   brands are producing higher quality clothing
   C   people want more choice in sportswear

Cambridge B2 First Listening

Practice test 4

Part 1

You will hear people talking in eight different situations. For Questions 1–8, choose the correct answer, A, B or C.

---

1. You hear two people discussing a problem. What do they agree to do?

    A see a mechanic
    B ignore the problem
    C check the internet

2. You hear a woman talking about her first job. What was her first job?

    A receptionist
    B nurse
    C doctor

3. You hear a man talking on the radio about fishing.
   The official reason for the fishing fines is:

    A to maintain fish supplies.
    B to keep fishermen safe.
    C to promote the local area.

4. You hear an interview with a football manager. What does she find most exciting?

    A the time before the game
    B seeing the players improve
    C watching the game develop

Transcripts on pages 114–115

Practice test 4

5. You hear two friends having an argument. What did the man do wrong?

   A he forgot something
   B he took something
   C he lost something

6. You hear a writer talking about her new book. What is she doing?

   A explaining where she got her ideas from
   B outlining the difficulty of being a writer
   C justifying the way she wrote the book

7. You hear a man talking about a concert he went to. How does he feel about it?

   A impressed by the musicians
   B annoyed it was so uncomfortable
   C pleased that he got tickets

8. You hear two friends talking about a new shop. What did they both dislike about it?

   A the clothes are expensive
   B the staff is unpleasant
   C the design is old-fashioned

Answers on pages 120–122

B2 Listening | Cambridge Masterclass

 P_4_2

Part 2

You will hear David, who is an adventurer, talking about going inside a volcano. For questions 9–18, complete the sentences with a word or short phrase.

David was **(9)**_____ to go into a volcano.

David had a difficult walk to the **(10)**_____.

It's possible to get a **(11)**_____ directly to the mouth of the volcano.

David was surprised by the **(12)**_____ on his way to the volcano.

The guides gave a **(13)**_____ which David thought was essential.

David compares the lift to the type that **(14)**_____ use.

People who go inside the volcano might be worried about the **(15)**_____ as you enter.

Once inside the volcano, they had to remain on the **(16)**_____.

When they returned to the top, David had some **(17)**_____.

The emptiness of the volcano is a **(18)**_____.

Transcripts on pages 116–118

Fractice test 4

 P_4_3

Part 3

You will hear five short extracts in which people are talking about how they help to protect the environment. For questions 19–23, choose from the list (A–H) why each person does it. Use the letters only once. There are three extra letters which you do not need to use.

A   For the future of the planet.

B   For their own children.

C   To make where they live nicer.

D   To set an example to others.

E   Because they are told to do it.

F   To stop waste.

G   Because it's the right thing to do.

H   To save wildlife in their area.

Speaker 1: 19
Speaker 2: 20
Speaker 3: 21
Speaker 4: 22
Speaker 5: 23

Answers on pages 120–122

Part 4

You will hear a radio interview with a psychologist called Rachel talking about why people enjoy theme parks. For Questions 24–30, choose the best answer (A, B or C).

24. When did Rachel get into the area of theme-park psychology?

  A after realising it was a well-paid area
  B after going to a famous theme park
  C after seeing a talk at a conference

25. Why do families tend to go to theme parks?

  A to create memories
  B to prevent boredom
  C to strengthen bonds

26. One study found that most people go on scary rides to:

  A impress their friends.
  B feel the excitement.
  C experience stress.

27. What do people generally think about long waiting times?

  A they make the ride more popular
  B they build up the excitement
  C they put people off visiting

28. What does Rachel say about the colours of theme parks?

    A they are tailored to certain areas
    B they are bright and energetic throughout
    C they think about the customers' desires

29. How do theme parks encourage visitors to the shop?

    A by controlling the air-conditioning
    B by putting children's items at the front
    C by positioning them near exits

30. How does she summarise visiting a theme park?

    A the visitor uses all their senses
    B the visitor is never in control
    C the visitor is the priority

Practice test 1: Transcript | Part 1 (pages 66–67)

Extract 1

Man Your daughter is making really good progress this year so far, and I'm really pleased.

Woman That is good news. I was worried that you were going to tell me something negative like she's always distracting the others or something.

Man Oh no! Overall, she's great to teach and I'm impressed with her ability to get on well with the other students in her class. She's quite confident and enjoys helping her classmates on projects. However, she could pay attention a bit more when I explain what we're doing. Sometimes, she makes mistakes and I think it's because of that.

Woman Okay. Well, we'll discuss this at home with her and see what we can do.

Extract 2

Woman You know, I'd definitely recommend that hotel to anyone traveling on business.

Man Absolutely. I mean, I know that the restaurant wasn't open when we arrived, but we knew it wouldn't be. I just couldn't believe that the receptionist had a list of all the local places printed out and ready for us!

Woman And remember when I couldn't print out my presentation for the meeting and someone drove to a printing shop for me?

Man Yes! I know it wasn't very far away, but they didn't have to do it. In a lot of hotels these days service isn't very good because the staff aren't allowed to make their own decisions on the spot like that.

Extract 3

I love growing tomatoes because their flavour is so much better than those you buy in the supermarkets. The key to growing successful tomatoes is to monitor them because they need a lot of water and sun. If your plants don't seem to be developing and getting stronger, you might need to move them. I plant several varieties of seeds in different parts of the garden in springtime and also some in plant pots because the soil in my garden isn't great. Every morning and evening during the growing season I check for insects and see which plants are dry. It's important to look for other clues like brown leaves too.

Extract 4

We have to increase renewable energy in this part of the country. But in my mind wind farms aren't as efficient as other sources such as solar. If the government gave us all some money to install solar panels on our roofs, it would be great. I mean, they don't take up as much space as wind farms. Also, I know plenty of people who would prefer wind farms not to be built in residential areas – they're always complaining about that. I wonder if they would be happier with solar instead? Especially if the local government helped out with the costs.

Extract 5

Woman	How can I help you today, sir?
Man	I'm looking for something smart to wear to a business event, but I don't want something too formal so perhaps a light colour?
Woman	What about this jacket over here? The style is very popular these days, especially with young executives aiming to give a good impression without coming across as too formal.
Man	It's very stylish, but I'm not sure I can afford it at the moment. It's just outside my price range, even though I'd love to have something like that in my wardrobe.
Woman	Okay, well we do have some similar styles I can show you which might be more affordable. Come over here…

Extract 6

The mayor's office has announced that the proposal for a new shopping centre has been approved. There was a lot of discussion about the location, and the initial suggestion of the site behind the train station was rejected. This was because the site is actually quite small. The construction company said that they wanted to provide plenty of parking. So, they finally persuaded the mayor's office that the best place for that was on the outskirts of the town. Even though it's a little further for customers to travel, businesses say that they are happy with the decision. They are going to build a children's playground as well as lots of parking.

Extract 7

Woman	You know, I wasn't sure if I would enjoy all these exercise classes when I joined the gym.
Man	I know what you mean. I thought they were pretty hard when I started, but they are definitely helping me get fit and I've noticed that I'm able to run more quickly than before.
Woman	That's great. I've been lifting some weights as well as doing the classes. I really believe that it'll help develop my muscles. I've already lost quite a lot of weight, but I still feel weak and so that's what I'm focusing on now.
Man	Well, I hope you start noticing a difference soon.
Woman	Me too!

> Be prepared to hear some or all the options, either directly or indirectly.

Extract 8

Woman	Since I joined a few months ago, I can't believe how many interesting local people I've got to know.
Man	Yeah, so have I – although I wasn't expecting that. My motivation was driven by the fact that I'd realised that I needed to discover new authors and not just read the same thing all the time.
Woman	I decided to sign up for it so that I'd have more opportunities to talk about the things I was reading. My family don't really like talking about books very much, so I wanted to find some people like me.
Man	Well, it sounds like it was a great decision for both of us.

Practice test 1: Transcript | Part 2 (page 68)

Extract

Welcome to Lake Havasu City, Arizona! Today, I'm going to tell you about our famous bridge, London Bridge. Now, I know what you're thinking – London Bridge? Shouldn't that be in England, not Arizona? Well, it used to be in London, but American businessman, Robert P. McCulloch, bought the bridge and moved it all the way here! It might seem strange to sell a bridge, but unlike many people had thought, the English didn't do it for money. It simply couldn't carry the weight of traffic on it anymore, so they had to replace it, and… get rid of the old one!

Now, this isn't actually the very first London Bridge. It has been rebuilt several times over hundreds of years. In fact, the bridge before this one had shops and houses on it. It seems dangerous, doesn't it? In fact, the problem was that it was narrow – there wasn't the space for many larger forms of transport to cross it, and so they built a larger bridge. This was in the 1830s. After 130 years of use in London, it was bought by McCulloch in the 1960s and it was officially opened in Arizona in the 1970s. At that time, Lake Havasu City was incredibly small. It had around 20 properties and just a handful of local people. This was largely because it was desert, and miles away from the major cities. But McCulloch had big plans. He was a housing developer and wanted to make the area popular, both with tourists, but also with retired people who he wanted to encourage to move there. His plan worked. Now, more than 50,000 people live in the city, and more than a million visitors come to see the bridge every year. That's a great number!

Interestingly, when they rebuilt the bridge here, they didn't rebuild it exactly. The internal structure, built originally in stone, was replaced with steel. This meant the bridge could be lighter but also stronger – but the stonework on the outside is all original. Also, the decision on where to build the bridge is quite interesting. Obviously, in London, the bridge crossed the famous Thames River, but here it wasn't built over a river but on land between the city centre and Pittsburgh Point. Some time after its building they redirected a canal through it, making Pittsburgh Point an island!

Now, let's take a look at the bridge… It's obviously a grey colour, but it's actually green too! This is because of the yellow LED streetlamps, which while keeping the traditional look use much less electricity than the old ones. We also celebrate special days by lighting the bridge up! For example, this evening it will be purple to celebrate a special football event in the city. I should also mention life on the bridge – obviously, no people live on it but plenty of other things do. People often see bats around the bridge, but the most common animals we see are birds. This is really great for the city, because, as you can imagine, in a desert there aren't many places for such animals to go. We also had a wild cat living inside the bridge for a few months too!

For many years now, this bridge has been the pride of the city. And we hope it will be with us for many hundreds of years to come. With the desert conditions, where there isn't much humidity or cold, the bridge requires little maintenance, and so it should last for years!

So, that's the end of the tour. There's plenty to do in town, if you'd like to have a look around. And if you'd like to go on a boat ride, you can get tickets in the visitor centre, which is right next to the bridge. They're only $2 and it's well worth it in my opinion.

Practice test 1: Transcript I Part 3 (page 69)

Extract 1

I moved to this village about two years ago and thought there would be a great sense of community in a smaller place, but actually, things were better in the city! Most of the time here, I don't even see another person in the street! It's so quiet. I suppose, when I go to the bakers or the post office, the staff in there always have time for a chat, and that hardly ever happened where I used to live. Also, I don't spend as much money as I used to either. That's probably a good thing. Perhaps I'm just not ready for the slower pace of life. I will hopefully get used to it in time.

Extract 2

Oh, I'm definitely glad I made the move to the countryside. It feels much healthier than being in the city, and, well, there's just more space to live. It does take me longer to get to work, though. It's about an hour on the train, but it's very reliable and I don't mind much because I just spend that time watching movies on my phone. Although the travel takes longer, I'd recommend living in the countryside to anyone, as long as they enjoy peace and quiet like me. It's perhaps not a life for people who like lots of excitement, but I find my life has improved in so many ways.

Extract 3

Moving to the countryside really opened my eyes to a different way of living. When I lived in the city, I was always out and about with my friends going to the cinema or restaurants, but we don't have any of those services here in the village. Instead, I spend a lot of time with my neighbours. We share the food we grow in our gardens and make sure we check up on the elderly people who live alone. I love being part of this, and now I wish I'd made more of an effort to be friendly when I lived in the city.

Extract 4

As much as I'm delighted to be living here because it's quiet and my neighbours are all really friendly, the village would benefit from having a bus service, or maybe a couple of shops or a café. We have to drive to the nearby town if we want to do any shopping. It's not very far, so it doesn't take long, but in my view more people would come to live here if we had a bit more to offer. Anyway, I'm happy overall because I was really fed up with the city. My commute was over an hour and travelling by train had become so expensive.

Extract 5

I left the city a few years ago and opened a bakery in a village in the countryside. Living here was quite a shock at the beginning, because I missed going to the theatre and seeing my friends who all still lived in the city, but I soon got used to it. I think the thing that has changed most for me is that I don't spend nearly as much as I used to. I mean, there are very few shops near me, so I do different things and I grow a lot of my own food now which means I go the supermarket less.

Practice test 1: Transcript | Part 4 (pages 70–71)

Extract

Man	Welcome to 'The Natural Beauty Show', Emily. Could you tell us more about why you started making your own skincare products?
Woman	Sure. And thanks for having me. I have a degree in biology, so I know quite a lot about plants and which ones are good for the skin. When my son was younger, he suffered from spots on his face and neck. Being a teenager, he was very embarrassed, and I thought I should try to do something about it. We'd tried lots of products before, but they were extremely expensive. So, I thought: why not try making something myself? They were successful for my son and soon his friends wanted some. Soon after that, I set up the business.
Man	What challenges did you experience when you started the business?
Woman	I know many small businesses say marketing is tricky, but this was okay for me because my son and his friends had already spread the word about my products. I'd had great feedback from all these teenagers, and everyone wanted more. That was the problem – I was so busy making skincare products that I didn't have time to

	explore other ideas. I wanted to read more about different plants, but I just couldn't.
Man	Hmm, did you manage to find a solution to this problem?
Woman	Well, lots of different people gave me advice, and my manager from my old job told me that I had to employ someone to make the products so that I could free up some time for the other parts of the business. I joined a club for small businesses in my area, and through them I found my first employee! I much prefer chatting with other businesspeople in this group to using online groups. It's more personal.
Man	Can you tell us about your typical day?
Woman	I start the day by replying to customers who aren't happy with our products. It isn't a nice job, so I always get it out of the way first. Then I can do something much more fulfilling – working on the text for the skincare products' packaging. People don't realise how much of a difference it makes. Oh, and of course, we have to comply with regulations for legal purposes. At the end of the day, we have a staff meeting to chat about how things are going and spend some time together.
Man	Do you have any recommendations for people who are thinking of starting a small business?
Woman	Hmm. There's so much information online these days, which is a great help. As far as I'm concerned, though, it's essential to find someone who you trust to do your finances. And someone professional as well. Friends and family can be good sources of recommendation in this area because lots of people need to use an accountant for personal things as well as business.
Man	Why do you think your products have become so popular?
Woman	I think it mostly comes down to the fact that I'm a biologist. Customers trust my knowledge and know that the ingredients in the products are used because there is evidence that they work. I mean, there are cheaper skincare ranges for skin problems – but some of them contain chemicals that might cause other issues, even if they do clear up spots.
Man	Finally, Emily. What is your view on the future of natural skincare products?
Woman	That's a good question! A current trend is adding a lot of vitamins and minerals to creams, but this probably won't last long. The focus is more likely to be on increasing the amount of packaging made from biodegradable materials. I mean, most companies are moving towards doing this now. There will probably be more and more interest in using organic ingredients, but this is less appealing to customers compared to packaging.
Man	Thank you, Emily. And that's all we have time for today…

B2 Listening | Cambridge Masterclass

Practice test 2: Transcript | Part 1 (pages 74–75)

Extract 1

Man	So, what did you think of it?
Woman	It was okay, but there were far too many people attending.
Man	Did you think?
Woman	Yes, it felt like some kind of conference session rather than a paid course. Fifty people is too many!
Man	I suppose that's true, but I still thought it was very useful. I think it's essential to learn presentation skills like that, and we've got lots to take home.
Woman	Yes, that's true. I think it was good overall. I just think in the feedback I'll mention that I think thirty should be the maximum size.

Extract 2

When the match ends, please remember that there are only three main exits: the East Exit, the Central Exit and the Durham Exit. The West Exit, which is normally for families to leave the stadium, is closed today due to building work outside the gate. We advise anyone with children to remain in their seats until the majority of spectators have left the stadium. If you are unsure of how to exit, staff will be in the stadium and will be happy to help. Please make sure you take all your rubbish with you when you leave the stadium and please do not run.

Extract 3

Woman	Excuse me. I'd like to take this phone back please. It's not working properly.
Man	I'm sorry about that. What's wrong with it exactly?
Woman	Well, I kept thinking the screen has turned off, but it seems that the phone has actually switched itself off.
Man	Hmmm. Do you think it's getting too hot?
Woman	It doesn't feel too hot. I think it's just not powering up properly.
Man	We'll check it out. Would you like a refund for it or a replacement?
Woman	Can I replace it with a different phone? I saw a cool phone near the entrance that looks great.
Man	Yes, of course.

> If you find one question very hard, move on and come back to it later.

Extract 4

Man	I can't believe we're back at work tomorrow!
Woman	Yes, the holiday has ended too soon! But wasn't it nice?
Man	Yes, and the food was much better than I expected. In fact, I think I've put on weight!
Woman	Ha ha! Well, that often happens on holidays! If only we'd stayed in a different hotel, though.
Man	I know what you mean. It just needed a bit of decoration, didn't it? And some entertainment! But I'd definitely go back to the same resort. It had something for everyone.
Woman	Yes, even though we spent most of the days in the rain, it didn't seem to matter.
Man	Oh, it wasn't so bad. There were only a few days of bad weather.

Extract 5

I recently went to see 'Dust Bowl Mountain' at the cinema, and it was a pleasant surprise for me. It wasn't the usual kind of action film – it had a lot of emotion to it. The film was actually based on a book, but I don't necessarily think that means a film will be good. However, one of my fellow film buffs suggested that I see it, so I went in open-minded. He told me the director had done an excellent job with the film, and now I agree. I think I'll look out for more of his films in the future.

Extract 6

I suppose, when I went into the police force I thought it would be similar to what it's like when you see police on the TV. But I was surprised. I actually spend most of my days just walking around the streets talking to people. It's actually a lot less scary than I thought it might be. And there are lots of different jobs to do in the day. In fact, you've got to have writing skills and computer skills, so it's not perhaps as simple as it seemed to me at first. Still, most days are quite interesting, and I've gotten to know people in the community too!

Extract 7

I spend around an hour every day in the car travelling to and from work. I used to quite enjoy it, but I like it less and less these days. First, I struggle to see on the motorway at night. The lights to me just make things blurry, and don't help me to see the roads, but what drives me mad is when someone moves along at the speed of a snail and you're stuck behind them. It just makes me late, and I hate arriving late to work as I can never find a spot to park… it gets so busy in the mornings.

Extract 8

Looks are important. And sometimes we all need a little help. But never fear – you're not alone! At Shine-nez, we're the specialists at making your place look great! Just call us now on 0560 65 65 65 and take the stress out of your day. No job is too big or too small. We charge by the square metre. See our price list on our website shine-nez.com and quote the code SHINERADIO, that's SHINERADIO, for 10% off your booking. Remember, let us take on the hard work while you just Shine! Contact Shine-nez now on 0560 65 65 65.

Practice test 2: Transcript | Part 2   (page76)

Extract

Hello and welcome. I'm Hugo Mitchell. I work in road safety, which is why I am here to talk to you today. Before I start, I'm not focusing on drivers in this talk. I'll mainly be looking at how we can all walk the streets safely. Pedestrians need to be much more careful than other road users, so it's important that we all know what we should do.

I've worked in this area for ten years, so I hope you will find this talk useful. As well as my own knowledge, I'll look at data from surveys of over twelve towns, so we can see what's working and what isn't. In fact, I'd like to start with that.

We all need to take care when walking on the streets, but there are some areas where we need to be more careful. These areas are known as accident black spots. They are where accidents are more likely to happen. From the data, accidents are twenty times more likely to happen when people are going across the road without using a crossing. So, that's a key thing to remember – always cross where you are supposed to. But you still need to be careful. Even if you want to cross the road at some traffic lights, it's not enough to wait for the lights to change colour. Try and make eye contact with the driver coming near you. Make sure they can see you and are slowing down *before* you start walking.

Time of day is also important to think about. More accidents happen at night, mainly because of the eyesight of drivers and how well people can be seen. So, think about bright clothing if you go out in the evenings, and try to stay near streetlights. Also, never wear earphones when walking at night.

Another big factor is whether the streets have pavements. A road without pavements is five times more dangerous.

Road planning by councils helps lower risk, of course, but it's not enough. This all might seem like common sense to you, but the data shows that human error is by far the biggest reason accidents happen. Other factors, like mechanical or road faults, play a very small part in all this.

I also want to mention what the council has done to improve safety of *all* road users. They've been thinking a lot about making pavements safe. Streetlights have been installed in all of our major roads for years now, but they've also been planting trees along pavements to make them safer. The council are also thinking about changing road signs. They're looking at adding flashing signs to some busy areas, so drivers will slow down and be more careful. I'm unsure about this myself. Some people think that lights will make signs more obvious, but this could also be distracting. I wonder what they will decide to do about this, especially considering how much these lights cost.

So, what's in the future for road safety? Well, technology plays a big part. Self-driving cars will change everything, but will take a while to become common. One thing that is already available and popular is the Driver Attention Monitor, or D.A.M., in cars. This can tell us about tiredness and bad driving, and these things use something called artificial intelligence, or AI. This will make a big difference to safety. AI is often looked at with suspicion by the general public. However, for us in the safety industry, it could lead to almost zero accidents. And I'd like to think that's what everyone wants, really.

Practice test 2: Transcript | Part 3 (page 77)

Extract 1

I was actually terrible at art at school. I had no skill at all – but I always enjoyed it, even though I didn't pass the subject. When I was in my 40s, I decided to take a course and try again. I'd been working as an accountant for years, and I'd got a little bored in my job and just wanted to do something completely new and fun. I've got to say it's been incredible. The people there are so supportive, and I've learnt that actually I'm not so bad at art! I don't think I'll ever be Van Gogh, but it's certainly turned into a new hobby now!

Extract 2

Actually, I'm already an artist. I used to do it as a hobby, but it slowly grew into a job for me as I sold more and more pieces. Being successful doesn't stop me learning, though. I was self-taught, so I took a class because I doubted myself and my skills a little bit. I found out that I *was* doing things correctly, but, most importantly, I felt better about myself at the end. I think I was always worried that I wasn't properly trained, but now I feel ready to take any opportunity that comes my way in life!

Extract 3

I remember doing lots of art projects at school and always enjoying them, but, like many people, art wasn't a big part of my adult life. I actually came back to it when I retired, as although my life was quite relaxing it was also a little boring! I wanted to fill in some spare time with something new. I persuaded a group of friends to take an art class with me, and we had a fantastic time – and I learnt so many new skills! I've also now got the opportunity to show some of my art in the local town hall. I'm not sure I'm brave enough to do it, though, to be honest!

Extract 4

Art is an important part of my life, but it's more a hobby for me than anything. When a friend said she loved my work and would like me to design something for her garden wall, well, I was honoured. I'd done some initial designs on paper, but I took a course about wall art, just to make sure I was using the correct materials. It really helped, and lots of people have said that they love it! I'm wondering now if I should turn this hobby into a career. Although, I think it's quite a competitive area, so I'm not sure I'll be good enough.

Extract 5

I used to love art, but I hadn't done it for a long time when I decided to take the course. I remember the first day feeling so uncomfortable – I knew nothing! But I knew I had to take the course as I had such a busy schedule – I wanted something to calm me down, and I could save time just for myself. That's difficult to do when you have three children! I've actually improved a lot, and I now help the kids with their art projects. I'm thinking of meeting up with a group of local artists soon, just to ask them what it's like to dedicate themselves to art full time, and maybe get ideas for the future!

Practice test 2: Transcript | Part 4 (pages 78–79)

Extract

Interviewer	Welcome to the show, Chris Walker and Louise Franklin. I'm delighted that you could join us today on 'Learning for Sport'. Before we talk about your jobs as instructors, can you tell our listeners how you got into rock climbing?
Woman	Well, Chris has been climbing ever since he saw a TV show about it when he was a teenager, but for me it's quite a recent hobby. A few years ago, I was having coffee with a friend and she started telling me about a book she'd read which was written by a female rock climber. Her achievements sounded amazing. At that time, I was looking for a challenge, so I thought I'd give it a try.
Interviewer	Rock climbing sounds great as a hobby, but what made you want to teach others how to do it – Chris?
Man	I've done a few courses over the years – some good, some not so good. On the last course I was particularly impressed with the instructor's technique. I learned a lot and realised that training to be an instructor is a great way to improve.
Woman	I couldn't agree more! I just wanted to be like the instructors at my local climbing club – they make everything look so easy. When I found out that I could go on a course and learn to be like them, it seemed like a logical choice.
Interviewer	What are the requirements to become an instructor?
Man	You need to take one of the qualifications offered by Mountain Training, the organisation in the UK and Ireland that manages six different instructor courses.

	The courses relate to different types of climbing – so, for example, some are for climbing on indoor walls and there are others for assisting rather than leading climbs. Whichever one you choose, you must demonstrate that you have enough experience otherwise they won't let you on the course. Remember that they want everyone to pass, so it's better to wait until you're definitely ready.
Interviewer	It sounds tough. What was it like on the course?
Man	I really enjoyed all the physical aspects, but I think that's because I was quite fit before I started. Unfortunately, I found out that I'm really bad at giving instructions to other people. I worked hard to improve that on the course and I'm much clearer now.
Woman	For me, it was more about managing my response to situations. When we were practising with beginners, I worried that some of them would never be able to master even the basics. But the course made me realise that's not true – as long as you have a good instructor! Now I enjoy helping people achieve their goals, whatever their level and however small their goals might be.
Interviewer	Do you have any suggestions for people who want to try rock climbing?
Woman	Don't just do one session because you might be a little afraid if you've never done any climbing before. The ropes and equipment can be confusing. Commit to a short course so you can see yourself improving and gaining in confidence. I think a lot of people give up before they've overcome that initial fear. These short courses are designed to give you a real taste of climbing without spending a lot of time and money.
Interviewer	Thank you, Louise, that's great advice. And Chris, how would you say that rock climbing has affected or influenced your life?
Man	Well, I mostly climb outside, and I think getting out in nature is something that we should all do more often. Also, helping others improve their climbing skills and allowing them to believe in themselves makes me feel content because it's really worthwhile.
Interviewer	Yes, I can imagine. Now I'd like to move on to…

B2 Listening | Cambridge Masterclass

Practice test 3: Transcript | Part 1 (pages 82–83)

Extract 1

Hi Daniel, it's Julia here. Unfortunately, I'm afraid I've got a bit of a problem right now. My daughter isn't feeling very well, and I think it would be best if I stayed home to look after her. I don't think it's serious enough to go to the doctors, but I'd rather not leave her alone. Anyway, that means I won't be able to make it for the tennis match later this evening. I was wondering if you're free on Friday instead? I know there are some free courts because I called the club earlier to check. Let me know what you think.

Extract 2

Man	I'm looking for a house which is near the local primary school because I have two young children and I'd like it if they could walk to school.
Woman	Okay. Well, we have a few options for you – some are large flats and others are houses.
Man	Okay, let me stop you there because I definitely want somewhere with a garden. Besides the children, we also have a large dog and it needs constant exercise. It's much easier to just let him outside rather than taking him to the park three times a day!
Woman	Okay, we have this house here. You can see from the photos that the garden is quite large – there's even space for a barbecue!

Extract 3

Where we are standing now formed part of the castle gardens. They were added during the 18th Century, but the castle itself is older. It was built a hundred years before that. As you can see, the gardens have different walled sections, which suggests that they were extended over the years. Although we are not sure, it is likely that this happened during the 19th Century when the castle was also extended. You can see that the walls built at this time were constructed from different-coloured bricks. Now, let's move on to the next part of the tour, the entrance to the castle…

Extract 4

Man	I've been looking at the travel options for the conference next week. Unfortunately, if we want to get there by 9.30 we're going to need to take the early train.
Woman	Okay, that's fine. I don't mind getting up early for a conference, but are you sure about getting the train? Isn't it expensive? Why don't we take the bus instead because it doesn't take that much longer?
Man	Well, I think the train is worth the money, to be honest, because it's much more comfortable. There's more room for your luggage and the seats are bigger. I mean, we have to pay extra if we want to reserve a seat, but I'd rather have a pleasant journey.

Extract 5

Woman I really hope it goes well after all the preparation we've done.

Man Well, I'm certain that the team will really enjoy it. We've put considerable time and effort into it, and I think that afterwards everyone will understand much more about the project and why it is essential for the company. Remember that everyone in the audience actually *wants* to hear what we have to say so there's no need to be nervous in my opinion.

Woman Well, I just hope that they think it's interesting and they ask some good questions at the end as that will make me feel like it was all worth it.

Extract 6

Man Do you think we should take the kids to the new pizza restaurant on Saturday night?

Woman I'm not sure. They've already eaten pizza once this week – remember, we had pizza delivered after their swimming class on Tuesday – so I think I'd prefer it if we had something a bit healthier.

Man We could get them to look up a new recipe and order the ingredients online. I think that would be a nice way to spend the evening together as a family, and we don't need to spend lots of money at a restaurant.

Woman Okay, that sounds like a better idea.

Extract 7

Man I was wondering if you'd like to come to the flower show that's taking place in Trenton next Saturday? I realised the other day that the summer food festival starts here tomorrow, which probably means the city centre will be full of tourists, so I was thinking of getting out of town while it's on.

Woman Ah, that sounds like it might be interesting. I'd planned to see something at the theatre on Saturday evening, but now I'm not convinced that's a great idea.

Man Okay, so how about I drive and pick you up at about ten o'clock, which will give us plenty of time to get there.

Woman Great. I'd really appreciate that.

Extract 8

I know lots of people think that students shouldn't be allowed to take their mobile phones into the classroom these days. They think it's a waste of time or that students will just be checking social media all the time. And yes, it's true that they can distract some students from their work, but this only happens if the teacher doesn't manage things properly. Mobile phones can be used for looking up facts and checking information, so they can actually help in lots of different ways. As long as teachers know how to get the best out of mobile phones, I don't have a problem with them in class.

Practice test 3: Transcript | Part 2

> Extract

Hi everyone. My name is Paula, and today I'm going to talk about video games – why people play them and what makes a good game. As someone who works in this area, I think I know something about the topic.

Lots of people have studied video games. And while psychologists say that a sense of connection often attracts people to playing them, it's not people's main motivation – that's the sense of achievement they get. There's nothing quite like succeeding in a game and making it to the next level! But gaming also produces lots of benefits, too. One example of this is that people often feel in a calm but concentrated state when they're playing, and this helps with stress levels. It can also take us away from everyday life.

Of course, there are so many types of games, so not all of these factors will apply to all games, but we certainly think about these kinds of things when making a game. Let me tell you how it's done. The first place that development starts is in the Concept Team. They really have the initial idea, and then my team, the art department, tries to think of the look and feel of the game.

Some initial drawings are done, and also we think about the technology we need. At this stage we also make a plan. We identify the competition and define the audience for the game. This is very important because the game design and the rules of the game will change depending on this.

We then work on making a test version of the game. This is just to see how it works. Then we show it to the managers. We wait for approval of the test version, and they tell us what the budget is and what changes they'd like, so we can start work on a complete version. We also get a suggested release date for the game here.

This leads us to the main production, and this is when all the hard work starts. There's a lot to be done before the game is ready to sell. It's a team effort between the designers and technical people. This isn't a series of stages, like many development projects – it's more like a cycle, with feedback and changes going from the design to the technical team and back again. Towards the end of production, the marketing team also starts working on the game. There used to be lots of huge adverts for new games, on things like movie trailers, but we tend to use social media instead these days. This means we can target advertising at people playing similar games. You can't do that in mass-media adverts, and it's also a lot cheaper!

Our company doesn't stop working when the game is sold, either. We've got a huge support team in two countries offering support in twelve different languages. Gamers get really annoyed if something isn't working for them, so this also helps us identify anything that needs to go back to the development team. There are always a couple of small errors that appear in the final product. We aim for none, because we want the game to sell well, be enjoyable and have few, if any, complaints.

And that's the end of the process really. Developing video games is a great job and I'd recommend it to everyone. It's so creative, for everybody that works in the company, and if your games are good it can be very well-paid! If you'd like more information about working in this area, and what qualifications you might need, please do ask me.

Practice test 3: Transcript | Part 3 (page 85)

Extract 1

I am a nursery schoolteacher, and I just love getting to know the children in the first year. They've never been away from their parents all day before, and it's interesting to see how they manage it. Some of them find it difficult to share toys, for example, while others really enjoy having new interactions. I always get a nice feeling when I work out the games and activities that interest each child. This is because it can have a big impact and help them settle into the whole-school environment. They know they've got something fun to do even if they're a bit nervous.

Extract 2

My work as a martial arts instructor gives me a lot of pleasure, especially in children's classes. We have to spend a lot of time helping students manage their emotions. Martial arts are all about control, and instructors need to understand that children do not think about this in the same way as adults. I spend a lot of time reading about how children's brains work so I can be a better instructor. We get different personalities, and some children are very sure of themselves while others can be very shy. It's important to get them all working together in classes so that they can *all* improve their skills.

Extract 3

I teach children who are 11 and 12 years old, and for me this is the best age group because they are about to become teenagers. You can start to see their characters taking shape at this age. Some are obviously confident and like to lead in class, whereas others are better at listening to their friends or problem-solving. It's so interesting watching them all interact with each other. At this age, school also starts to become more interesting because they have different classes for subjects like geography and history. I notice that they ask a lot more questions at this age!

Extract 4

I run an art club for young people on Saturday mornings. It's become really popular recently because quite a lot of parents think that the school curriculum is too academic these days. They want their children to have more time to do creative activities. A lot of the children want to make digital pictures using all sorts of different software, so I'm trying to get more confident using all this stuff. What I love is that the internet is full of ideas about how to use them in class. Last week I found a website full of games with some excellent instructions for teachers.

> Listen for synonyms and different ways to say the information in the options.

Extract 5

I am an educational psychologist, and I work with children who have learning difficulties. My job can be challenging, but people like me can make a big difference to families. I regularly communicate with parents, and it's great to explain the improvements that I've seen in their children's learning – it doesn't matter if they are small. All children have talents and abilities, but for some the traditional classroom just isn't the best place for them to learn. I have a lovely quiet room with toys and games. It's a place where children can learn about themselves and discover what they like to do.

Practice test 3: Transcript | Part 4 (pages 86–87)

Extract

Interviewer	Natasha Evans is the manager of a successful sports shop. Today she's going to tell us all about her role in the company and her views on selling sportswear. Welcome, Natasha. Tell me: what is your daily life like at work?
Woman	Well, my job covers all the usual things that you'd expect from a shop manager. I check and order stock, manage the staff and so on. But something that people might not expect, though, is that I have to make sure I know what's going on in the world of sport. The changing fortunes of teams and players effect what we stock in the shop. This changes from year to year. I read about it a lot, but I don't watch a lot of sport.
Interviewer	What's the age of most of your customers?
Woman	Teenagers and young people make up a large proportion of our customers. If you asked most people what modern teenagers are into, they'd probably say 'designer trainers'. And this is true to some extent, and what's most popular with this age group are names like Nike and Adidas. We sell more of those items than football shirts. Young people are the consumer group that dictates our stock, especially the quantities of things we buy for the different departments – sportswear, shoes, equipment and so on.
Interviewer	I imagine that selling sportswear is very competitive. How do you manage to keep your customers happy?
Woman	Well, most successful shops have a wide selection of items that are connected to popular sports like football and tennis and swimming. However, I think that listening to customers and getting to know them is what has made this shop stay profitable. For me, that's how you make sure customers keep coming back. It works better than having lots of discounts or loyalty cards.
Interviewer	Is there a part of the business which interests you from a personal perspective?
Woman	Yes, there is actually. I've recently started a business course which is very interesting. I didn't study business at university, and I'd like to update my skills and knowledge. Right now, we're focusing on the habits of different types of shoppers. After that we're going to study sustainability and the labour conditions

	in large factories around the world. I think the last one will be the most interesting for me.
Interviewer	And talking about working conditions, what are your staff like?
Woman	Oh, they are all great and work really well as a team. Some of them want to make a career out of working in sport. If they want to do this, going to conferences is vital – so we have a budget for that. Networking is great because they can meet inspiring people and get ideas for their future. Although I do sometimes have to remind them about the boring administrative tasks.
Interviewer	Is there any aspect of your job that you find challenging?
Woman	Despite the fact that we have a lot of regular customers – and I have a great team – planning is always a challenge. Things can change easily if someone is sick or we suddenly run out of an item. I've started using a planning tool on my laptop to predict possible problems and solutions.
Interviewer	And finally: do customers' tastes change a lot in sportswear like in other aspects of fashion?
Woman	Well, sportswear brands are becoming much more popular now. People wear them as a form as casual clothing now not just for playing sports. No one would have thought about doing this a few years ago. But beliefs about what clothing is appropriate for certain situations is not the same as it was.
Interviewer	Hmm. That's very interesting. Well, thank you, Natasha…

B2 Listening | Cambridge Masterclass

Practice test 4: Transcript | Part 1 (pages 90–91)

Extract 1

Man	Hmmm. I think we've got a problem with the car. What do you think this yellow light means?
Woman	I'm not too sure. It might be something connected to the engine? We should probably take it to a mechanic so they can check it.
Man	I'd rather not. I've got to take it to a meeting tomorrow – I've got to drive there – and we'll never get the car back from the mechanic in time.
Woman	Well, we can't ignore it. What if I just try to look it up online? Perhaps then we can see if it's serious problem or not.
Man	That sounds like a good idea. If it's bad, I promise I'll ask someone to look at it.

Extract 2

I remember how I felt on my first day at the job. I was so nervous! It's always hard when you start a job. You can't find anything, and you don't know what to do! But everyone around me was lovely. The nurses were so friendly and always offered me help when I needed it. Actually, it was working in the hospital then that persuaded me to study medicine. I mean, I was only answering enquiries and organising paperwork but working with the public like that made me realise that I really enjoyed helping people. Now, I've been a doctor for five years, and I absolutely love it.

Extract 3

It used to be much easier to go fishing in the area, but now there are fines if you fish in the wrong place. According to the local government, it's for our own safety but I don't think that's particularly true. I mean, we're still allowed out in boats to fish. That's far riskier than fishing on the shore. I understand that people think we need to maintain the number of fish in the sea, but wouldn't it be better to stop big companies that are fishing? I think the local government cares more about profits and how the area looks for tourists than us local fishermen.

Extract 4

Football management is a difficult job. There's a lot of money involved, and a lot of pressure. But nothing beats the excitement of match day. To me, it makes all the stress worth it. Lots of managers find the most exciting part is watching how the game changes, because obviously a big part of the job is making decisions during the match. But, for me, that time in the dressing room just before the match begins is particularly thrilling. What I say in that room can make players play better and make them believe in themselves. I think that this time can make a big difference.

Extract 5

Woman   I really cannot believe this! That novel was really special to me. I knew I shouldn't have given it to you in the first place!

Man   I'm honestly sorry. Look, it's got to be somewhere – these things don't just disappear.

Woman   When I gave it to you, I *did* tell you that I'd got it signed by the author, and it's been in my collection for years.

Man   I don't know what to say. I'll look again and if it doesn't turn up I'll get you a replacement.

Woman   Well, it's not going to be signed, is it? You may as well just forget it, but don't think I'm lending you anything else ever again!

Extract 6

I am pleased to be here today to talk about my newest novel *Flowers in Time*. Now, this book is quite different from my other novels, and I wanted to explain the reason behind this. For me, when I had the idea for the story I knew I had to write it outside of time order, so the novel jumps in time. One minute we see Jules, the main character, as a mother, the next as a teenager. This might make it a difficult read for some people, but I felt the story needed this, and I hope you agree once you read it.

Extract 7

I went to see the Brilston Quarter last week in the Central Hall. The tickets were half price for the last few days, so I thought: why not treat myself? It was much better than I'd expected, both in terms of the music and the musicians. You could really tell they were dedicated professionals, and they were absolutely spectacular in places. Although, I have to say they didn't look too comfortable under the lights of the stage. I think they were too hot – you could see them sweating! I'm glad I wasn't playing and was just relaxing in the audience.

Extract 8

Woman   People told me that the new shop in town is great, but I didn't think it was as good as it looks.

Man   I know what you mean. I went in last week, and it looks great from the outside, even though it's in that old building, but once you get in it's not very impressive. The shop assistants basically ignored me, and everything was so expensive too – and it didn't seem worth it.

Woman   Oh, I thought there were some cheap things in there, but I wouldn't buy anything. Not with the way they treat you in there.

Man   Yes, it's one of those kind of shops that thinks it better than its customers.

Practice test 4: Transcript | Part 2 (page 92)

> **Extract**

I'm always looking for new exciting challenges, so when I had the opportunity to go into a volcano, I knew I had to grab it. Most people perhaps wouldn't fancy doing something like that, and I can understand why people might get nervous about the idea. Not me, though. I was quite keen! And, after all, the volcano isn't active, so it's completely safe.

On my adventure, once I arrived at the nearest city, I took a bus to the parking area. From there I had a three-kilometre hike to the meeting point, which was next to the mouth of the volcano. It was quite a tricky walk to be honest because of the rocks, and I imagine it's easy to twist an ankle or something. The problem is the land isn't suitable for vehicles like cars, so it's walk or take a helicopter, which I didn't have the money for! And it's not any quicker than the hike when you take into account all the waiting around.

I managed to complete the walk in just under an hour. I wore good hiking boots, as I knew the land would be difficult. I didn't expect the changes in the weather, though. Preparation is really important, as one minute it's hot and the next you need to put on waterproofs – so you need to carry some different clothes, just so you're not caught by surprise.

At the mouth of the volcano, there's a group of guides who work there and will take you down. They fit you with the special equipment you need, like a harness, head lamp and helmet, but they also give you a safety talk, which was by far the most important thing. It prepared me for what I was about to do, and what to do if something goes wrong. If you go, I suggest you listen carefully to the guides.

There were four other visitors with me when I went. I expected us to go down in a lift like the ones that miners use in mines, but actually it was more like a lift for window cleaners. It was completely open with the volcano all around it. You could see everything! It was absolutely stunning.

I would definitely recommend doing this, even people with a fear of heights! It might sound strange, but you do feel completely safe. The one thing that might put people off, though, is the lack of room at the mouth of the volcano. The entrance is really quite small, but once you get inside, the volcano opens up into a massive space! And when you're down there, it's unlike any place you've ever been. We were allowed out of the lift at this point. I was worried that we'd have to stay in the group, all together and just listen to the guide, but actually, we could take photos and walk around – as long as we didn't leave the marked paths. My pictures don't really show how amazing the rocks were. There were all kinds of colours down there.

On the journey back up, I felt sad to be leaving and quite cold. Some of the guides were waiting for us at the top with hot lamb soup or hot chocolate. As I'm a vegetarian, I only had the latter – but it was so needed. It was actually quite cold and wet inside the volcano, so it was nice to have something to warm me up.

So, it was a really special experience, and so unusual. Most volcanoes close up so you can't enter them, but thankfully this one is empty. Nobody knows why it's open inside – it remains a mystery. But it's a treasure of natural beauty, and I feel very lucky that I have seen it.

Practice test 4: Transcript | Part 3 (page 93)

Extract 1

We know much more about global environmental concerns compared to our parents, and I try to do my best to help. There are lots of environmental projects here, and I try to take part in as many as I can. For example, me and my kids help pick up rubbish around the village and I help plant new trees. I think it's really important to take part in things like this to ensure your local environment stays pleasant. I believe if you think of that first, then eventually it will make the whole world a better place. That's really what we all want!

Extract 2

I do my best to protect the environment, but I worry it's not enough. I'm always concerned how what we throw away goes into nature, especially the oceans, and I'm sick of seeing plastic in the streets. That's why I do my best to use up everything I have; I always use things that are recyclable and I also try to buy second-hand if I can. I also try to encourage others in the community to do the same thing, although I don't think they always listen. I suppose some people see it as a big effort to help the environment.

Extract 3

We often recycle at home, and we've also got an electric car. I don't really enjoy recycling things – it's so annoying having all those different bins – but my husband and kids say it's the right thing to do, so I just do it. Electric cars are just the most popular ones to buy these days – in my circle of friends, anyway. For us, it's actually turned out cheaper to run than our old car, which is an advantage. It's also much less noisy than the old car. I remember the days when cars polluted a lot – you could even feel it when you breathed – so things have become so much better really.

Extract 4

I try to do my best to help the environment, although I'm sure it's not enough. I'm not always very good at recycling, for example. I do, however, bike everywhere and I never take a plane – so I don't think I pollute the environment very much. Now I'm a dad, I think it's important to think about this kind of thing – mainly for my daughters and their future families. I think my parents' generation didn't do much at all, and now we're starting to see the effects of that. It would be a shame if my generation didn't do enough either.

Extract 5

There are so many different ways we can care for the environment, and it's hard to do everything. I think we've just got to do small things that make a difference. I try to encourage bird species in my garden, because I know some of their populations are in trouble. My children also love helping me with this – it's such a great family activity! Of course, lots of people choose to reduce their waste or save energy, and these are great things to do too. I'm more concerned with waste in general, but I think it's such a big issue that it's hard to know where to start!

Practice test 4: Transcript | Part 4 (pages 94–95)

Extract

Interviewer	Today, I'm talking to Rachel Parkinson, who's a theme-park psychologist. I didn't even know that was a job! So, Rachel, what made you decide to specialise in theme parks?
Woman	Well, I'd always been a theme-park fan, but I'd also been interested in psychology. When I saw a talk that someone did on entertainment psychology at a conference, I realised I could combine those two things. And I'm glad I did. It's really interesting, and the field has excellent pay and conditions.
Interviewer	So, why do people go to theme parks?
Woman	For lots of different reasons, really. Groups of friends tend to go because it strengthens their relationships, but parents often take their children so they can all have something to look back on. It's nice to think back to a really fun day, and I've got to say, theme parks *are* a lot of fun for everyone!
Interviewer	Well, yes, they are fun, but they can also be quite terrifying. Especially the big rides, don't you think?
Woman	Well, I'm not so scared of them to tell you the truth. To me they're really exciting, and some of those rides are truly impressive. But did you know that recent research shows that most people go on them because they are stressful, but in a positive way. They make us feel really good afterwards, and actually boost our mood!
Interviewer	But it's the waiting and thinking about what's going to happen. I'm afraid it's not for me. In fact, I've known people waiting for those big rides for hours! Why do people bother?
Woman	Ha ha! Well, actually the parks design the waiting times, because it makes the rides look like they're popular. You would think it would make people decide to not go on the ride, and try something else, but actually psychology shows they enjoy the tension of thinking – just like you: what's going to happen!? Of course, there does need to be a limit to that waiting time, and we always try to make sure people aren't put off.
Interviewer	Hmm. That's really fascinating. What else can you tell us about theme-park psychology?
Woman	Well, one interesting thing is the use of colours that are used. We always think quite carefully about this. Red shows excitement and aggression, but soft blues, greens and greys give people a feeling of calm. We make sure we use these

	colours in the right places, so customers feel more, or less, energetic, depending on if they're at the rides or near, say, the café or shops.
Interviewer	Talking about the shops. I imagine they make theme parks a lot of money. Are they also considered carefully?
Woman	You'd be surprised how much we think about the customers' shopping experience. Children tend to always want to go into the shops, so we always make sure there's plenty of toys around, but we also want customers to buy things before they leave. Some theme parks actually lower the temperature in the shops if they want to sell more expensive items like coats and jackets. And it works! These kinds of sales can make a big difference.
Interviewer	Wow! That's incredible. So, how would you sum up the experience of visiting a theme park?
Woman	We think carefully about the visitor experience, but this is for business purposes. We manage absolutely everything. People think they are making choices, but we've kind of designed everything so we know exactly what they're going to do. Our priority is the success of the park, but of course we want people to have a great experience, full of sounds, fun and emotions too. It's always important that they come back!

Answers

Practice test 1 (pages 65–71)

Part 1

1 A   2 C   3 A   4 B   5 B   6 B   7 B   8 A

Part 2

9 (weight of) traffic
10 narrow
11 1970s / nineteen-seventies
12 retired people
13 steel
14 land
15 special days
16 birds
17 (desert) conditions
18 boat ride

Part 3

19 E   20 H   21 B   22 G   23 F

Part 4

24 C   25 B   26 C   27 C   28 A   29 B   30 A

Practice test 2 (pages 73–79)

Part 1

1 B   2 A   3 A   4 C   5 B   6 A   7 A   8 C

Practice test answers

Part 2

9	pedestrians	14	human error
10	surveys	15	planting trees
11	crossing	16	distracting
12	eye contact	17	Driver Attention Monitor / DAM
13	Bright clothing	18	safety industry

Part 3

19 G 20 H 21 C 22 E 23 A

Part 4

24 C 25 C 26 A 27 B 28 A 29 B 30 C

Practice test 3 (pages 81–87)

Part 1

1 B 2 C 3 A 4 B 5 A 6 C 7 A 8 C

Part 2

9	achievement	14	cycle
10	everyday life	15	social media
11	art department	16	languages
12	audience	17	errors
13	budget	18	well-paid / well paid

Part 3

19 D 20 B 21 A 22 G 23 F

Part 4

24 B 25 C 26 A 27 B 28 C 29 C 30 A

Practice test 4 (pages 89–95)

Part 1

1 C 2 A 3 B 4 A 5 C 6 C 7 A 8 B

Part 2

9 (quite) keen
10 meeting point
11 helicopter
12 (changes in the) weather
13 safety talk
14 window cleaners
15 lack of room
16 (marked) paths
17 hot chocolate
18 mystery

Part 3

19 C 20 F 21 E 22 B 23 H

Part 4

24 C 25 A 26 C 27 B 28 A 29 A 30 B

www.ingramcontent.com/pod-product-compliance
Lightning Source LLC
Chambersburg PA
CBHW051316110526
44590CB00031B/4369